MW01029352

"In *The Four Last Thi[ngs]...* ful guide to help us [...] with God. Well researched and concisely written, his book is a must-read on a topic too often avoided by too many. No one will escape death, but all will benefit immensely in preparing for it by reading and meditating on the messages of Fr. Menezes' excellent book."

— Most Rev. Robert J. Baker, S.T.D.
Bishop of Birmingham, Alabama

"By reminding us of the Four Last Things, Fr. Menezes summons us to hope for the ultimate good of spending eternity with God and reminds us of a proper fear to avoid condemnation in Hell. He urges us to live this life with that love of God and neighbor that prepares us for eternal life of love, and to avoid all hatred, which would only prepare us for the isolating hatred in Hell. Contemporary culture entertains itself with immortality if it includes hideous devouring zombies or beautiful blood-sucking vampires. Fr. Menezes calls us to the beauty of immortality in the image and likeness of God."

— Fr. Mitch Pacwa, S.J.

"We all wonder what will come when we draw our last breath of life, and in this profoundly important book Fr. Wade Menezes draws back the veil of mystery to give us insight and instruction about the ultimate *final* four — death, judgment, Heaven, Hell. With skill and precision, he weaves together Sacred Scripture, Church teaching, and the wisdom of the saints to encourage us to strive for the ultimate prize — life on high in Christ Jesus for all eternity.

Concise and straightforward, this book filled me with hope and joyful anticipation of what is to come! May it do the same for you!"

—Johnnette S. Benkovic
EWTN, Host and Author
Founder and Director, Women of Grace®

"Since when do we go on a long journey and never talk about our destination? In his new book, my brother priest Fr. Wade Menezes helps us focus on where life's journey takes us all, and he does it in a way that shows us what 'new evangelization' means. He takes the timeless truths of the Faith and presents them in a new, joyful, fresh way that spurs us to accept the gift of salvation!"

—Fr. Frank Pavone
National Director, Priests for Life

The Four Last Things

p. 80 — quote (2)

Fr. Wade L.J. Menezes, CPM

The
FOUR
LAST
THINGS

A Catechetical Guide to
Death, Judgment, Heaven, and Hell

EWTN PUBLISHING, INC.
Irondale, Alabama

Nihil Obstat: Colin B. Donovan, S.T.L., *Censor Librorum*
Imprimatur: Robert J. Baker, S.T.D., *Bishop of Birmingham in Alabama*
June 4, 2017, Solemnity of Pentecost
Cum permissum superiorum.

EWTN Publishing, Inc.
5817 Old Leeds Road, Irondale, AL 35210

Distributed by Sophia Institute Press, Box 5284, Manchester, NH 03108

Library of Congress Cataloging-in-Publication Data
Names: Menezes, Wade L. J., author.
Title: The four last things : a catechetical guide to death, judgment,
   heaven, hell / Fr. Wade L.J. Menezes, CPM.
Description: Irondale, Alabama : EWTN Publishing, Inc., 2017. | Includes
   bibliographical references.
Identifiers: LCCN 2017030312 | ISBN 9781682780428 (pbk. : alk. paper)
Subjects: LCSH: Eschatology. | Catholic Church—Doctrines.
Classification: LCC BT821.3 .M46 2017 | DDC 236—dc23 LC record available at
https://lccn.loc.gov/2017030312

For my parents,
Louis and Joyce Menezes,
who taught me the Faith so well,
each in their own way

Contents

The Four Last Things

Introduction

Work out your own salvation with fear and trembling; for God is at work in you, both to will and to work for his good pleasure. Do all things without grumbling or questioning, that you may be blameless and innocent, children of God without blemish.

—Philippians 2:12–15

God created us without us; but he did not will to save us without us.

—St. Augustine, *Sermo* 169[1]

---

[1] Quoted in *Catechism of the Catholic Church* (CCC), no. 1847.

The purpose of this book is to shed light on the Four Last Things—a most important doctrine of Holy Mother Church rooted deeply in Sacred Scripture, Sacred Tradition, and the Magisterium. The Four Last Things is another way of describing the Church's *eschatology*, which comes from the Greek word *eschaton*, meaning "last," and refers to the study of the end of our earthly lives and the end of the whole world.

Throughout the text we will highlight pertinent passages from the universal *Catechism of the Catholic Church* that deal especially with each of the Four Last Things. My hope, then, is that this book will serve as a layman's catechetical guide to this important doctrine that is essential not just to our understanding of abstract theological principles, but to our pursuit of salvation itself. As St. Bernard of Clairvaux urges us: "Let us work for the food which does not perish—our salvation."[2]

Sadly, however, the doctrine of the Four Last Things has seemingly been forgotten since the Second Vatican Council. This surely is not the council's fault; Vatican II was a solid, faithful, orthodox council that was truly ushered in by the Holy Spirit. Rather, the Church's eschatology was deemphasized at the insistence of those who deemed the harder truths of death and judgment to be unappealing to modern men and women. And so the post–Vatican II Church *seemed* to highlight the reality of Heaven and salvation

[2] St. Bernard of Clairvaux, *Sermo de Diversis* 15.

THE FOUR LAST THINGS

at the expense of the Church's teachings on Death, Judgment, Purgatory, and Hell. But the fact is that Heaven and Hell, salvation and damnation, eternal life and eternal punishment are all *complementary* doctrines. They need each other to be complete; focusing only on the positive or only on the negative yields an unbalanced view of our world and the next.

Now, it is true that studying the Church's doctrine of the Four Last Things can be a troubling or even frightening undertaking. But before we let ourselves fall into that way of thinking, which I firmly believe can be a trap of the Evil One, let us look at a couple of passages from St. Paul:

> Rejoice in the Lord always; again I will say, Rejoice. Let all men know your forbearance. The Lord is at hand. Have no anxiety about anything, but in everything by prayer and supplication with thanksgiving let your requests be made known to God. And the peace of God, which passes all understanding, will keep your hearts and your minds in Christ Jesus. (Phil. 4:4–7)

> For God has not destined us for wrath, but to obtain salvation through our Lord Jesus Christ, who died for us so that whether we wake or sleep we might live with him. (1 Thess. 5:9–10)

St. Paul gives us great consolation in these passages. He's telling us, clearly, that we are to rejoice, that we are not to have anxiety, that we are to seek the peace of God through prayer and supplication, and that this same God has called us not to His wrath, but to salvation.

We are called, then, to study and to understand the Four Last Things with great joy and great trust in God's plan for our lives. He desires our salvation. What does the image of the Divine Mercy say at the bottom? "Jesus, I Trust in You." The Church's eschatology is meant to be a beautiful and consoling doctrine—not a daunting and laborious one—in which we are presented with the truths of salvation: that which can lead us to salvation and that which can pull us away from it.

Now, we know that there is a certain kind of fear that the Lord desires from us; after all, "fear of the Lord" is a gift of the Holy Spirit. But this is a fear rooted in love. St. Dorotheos of Gaza, the celebrated abbot, echoes this when he says:

> Perfect love ... leads a man on to perfect fear. Such a man fears and keeps to God's will, not for fear of punishment, not to avoid condemnation, but ... because he has tasted the sweetness of being with God; he fears he may fall away from it.[3]

In working out our salvation, we should have a filial fear of God, not a servile fear of Him. This is what the psalmist means when he writes, "The fear of the LORD is the beginning of wisdom; a good understanding have all those who practice it" (Ps. 111:10). St. Peter Chrysologus, an early Church bishop, echoes this teaching when he tells us, "God's desire [is] to be loved rather than feared."[4] And St. Francis de Sales eloquently and concisely states: "We must fear God out of love, not love Him out of fear."[5]

The doctrine of the Four Last Things, then, is not meant to frighten us. Rather, it is meant to lead us to live more faithful, committed Christian lives here on earth. This meditation from

---

[3] Quoted in Paul Thigpen, ed., *A Dictionary of Quotes from the Saints* (Ann Arbor, MI: Servant Publications, 2001), p. 89. *A Dictionary of Quotes from the Saints* will be hereafter abbreviated *DQS*.

[4] St. Peter Chrysologus, *Sermo* 108.

[5] Quoted in Carol Kelly-Gangi, ed., *The Essential Wisdom of the Saints* (New York: Fall River Press, 2008), p. 7. *The Essential Wisdom of the Saints* will be hereafter abbreviated *EWS*.

THE FOUR LAST THINGS

My *Daily Bread*, a devotional by Fr. Anthony J. Paone, S.J., sums up this truth beautifully:

> Few things in this earthly life are absolutely certain. The most undebatable of these is death. Every man, even the atheist, will admit this much — death is certain. Death, however, is not the very last event in this life of ours. Right after death, we shall be judged. Our private judgment will be repeated on the Day of Judgment when all men will know us for what we are.
>
> Our judgment will depend on how we live this earthly life of ours. If we have honestly done our best and have followed the commandments of Christ, we shall be rewarded with the perfect life of Heaven. If, however, we have disregarded His loving directions and refused to make use of His generous help, we shall be condemned to hell.
>
> Death, judgment, Heaven and hell — these are the four last things toward which we are moving each hour of the day and night. They will never frighten us if our conscience is clear. If we love God in our daily life, that is, if we are sincerely trying to know and follow His holy will, we have no reason to fear.
>
> By keeping this eternal goal ever before us, we shall think straight when life's problems and difficulties face us.... We must strive to become eternity-minded. We must seek to guarantee to ourselves, as far as is in our power, the unending success and unmarred happiness of Heaven.[6]

To ignore the Church's eschatology is not only to risk great harm to souls, but also to undercut the Church's essential message of faith. Pope St. John Paul II, in his 1984 Apostolic Exhortation

---

[6] Fr. Anthony J. Paone, S.J., *My Daily Bread*, introduction to bk. 1, pt. 1, sect. B.

Introduction

Reconciliatio et Paenitentia (Reconciliation and Penance), states this very clearly:

> Nor can the Church omit, without serious mutilation of Her essential message, a constant catechesis on what the traditional Christian language calls the four *last things of man*: death, judgment (universal and particular), hell and heaven. In a culture which tends to imprison man in the earthly life at which he is more or less successful, the pastors of the Church are asked to provide a catechesis which will reveal and illustrate with the certainties of faith what comes after the present life: beyond the mysterious gates of death, an eternity of joy in communion with God or the punishment of separation from him. Only in this *eschatological vision* can one realize the exact nature of sin and feel decisively moved to penance and reconciliation.[7]

To acknowledge and to believe in the Church's doctrine of the Four Last Things is to embrace the reality of eternity in our daily lives. But where will we spend this eternity—Heaven or Hell? This is why this topic must be of such importance to every person.

My hope, then, is that this book will aid you, with great joy and faithful determination, to learn, to accept, and to share the essential elements of the Church's eschatology. After all, this is part of our baptismal calling—bolstered by the Sacrament of Confirmation and sustained by regular reception of the sacrament of Confession and the sacrament of the Eucharist. We are all called to be students *and teachers* of the Faith.

There are two Scripture passages that I believe convey beautifully the truth that, regardless of one's vocation or state in life,

[7] St. John Paul II, Apostolic Exhortation *Reconciliatio et Paenitentia*, December 2, 1984, no. 26, emphasis added.

THE FOUR LAST THINGS

Almighty God exhorts us to live our lives virtuously and to "work out our salvation" so as to attain Eternal Beatitude for all eternity with Him:

> It is full time now for you to wake from sleep.... The night is far gone, the day is at hand. Let us then cast off the works of darkness and put on the armor of light. Let us conduct ourselves becomingly as in the day. (Rom. 13:11, 12–13)

> [May you] be filled with the knowledge of his will in all spiritual wisdom and understanding, to lead a life worthy of the Lord, fully pleasing to him, bearing fruit in every good work and increasing in the knowledge of God. May you be strengthened with all power, according to his glorious might, for all endurance and patience with joy, giving thanks to the Father, who has qualified us to share in the inheritance of the saints in light. He has delivered us from the dominion of darkness and transferred us to the kingdom of his beloved Son, in whom we have redemption, the forgiveness of sins. (Col. 1:9–14)

What beautiful commands and promises these are! They urge us on in this life to remain forever faithful to God and His Word as we strive for salvation in the next life.

St. Peter Chrysologus asks us a very important question: "Why do you ask how you were created and do not seek to know why you were made?"[8] We are created *for* the Beatific Vision—Heaven for all eternity with the Blessed Trinity—the God from Whom we come and to Whom we are called to return.

So let us heed this important calling, my friends, since knowing and embracing the doctrine of the Four Last Things prepares us to

---

[8] St. Peter Chrysologus, *Sermo* 148.

"work out our salvation" and at the same time to share it with others, which can be a powerful tool of evangelization to help others work out their own salvation as well.

Let us close this introduction and begin this book with a beautiful quote from St. Cyril of Jerusalem that should give us great confidence as we delve into our study of the Four Last Things:

> For if you believe that Jesus Christ is Lord and that God raised him from the dead, you will be saved and taken up to paradise by him, just as he brought the thief there. Do not doubt that this is possible. After all, he saved the thief on the holy hill of Golgotha because of one hour's faith; will he not save you too since you have believed?[9]

---

[9] St. Cyril of Jerusalem, *De Fide et Symbolo* 10–11.

Chapter 1

Death

There is ... a time to be born, and a time to die.

—Ecclesiastes 3:1, 2

There is a time to be born and a time to die. The fact that there is a natural link between birth and death is expressed very clearly in this text of Scripture. Death invariably follows birth and everyone who is born comes at last to the grave.

—St. Gregory of Nyssa, *Homily* 6, on Ecclesiastes

Animals die; insects die; plants die; and, yes, humans die—but only humans are rationally aware of that fact. This is because the human person is the only creature made in God's image and likeness. Only the human person is called to Eternal Beatitude—Heaven for all eternity. The human person comes from God and is called to return to God. Simply put, we are made in God's image and likeness to share, after this earthly life, in a life of eternal communion and happiness with Him.

> Truly no man can ransom himself, or give to God the price
> of his life, for the ransom of his life is costly, and can never
> suffice, that he should continue to live on for ever, and never
> see the Pit. (Ps. 49:7–9)

In other words, we cannot purchase eternal life, nor can we avoid death. So it is, then, that the doctrine of the Four Last Things is an essential doctrine that we must not take lightly. We know that one day each person will die, be judged, and receive either eternal reward or eternal reprobation. Our eternity will be one of salvation in heaven with Christ and the saints, or it will be one of punishment in Hell with the devils and the damned. The choice is ours to make by how we live right now.

The life expectancy in the United States is seventy-nine years. That may sound like a long time to some, and it represents an incredible increase in longevity over the course of the past few centuries. And yet, compared with the experience of eternity, it's nothing. We are barely infants in the scheme of our eternal destiny.

> Our years come to an end like a sigh. The years of our life are threescore and ten, or even by reason of strength four-score; ... they are soon gone, and we fly away. (Ps. 90:9–10)

> The time will come when you will wish that you had one more day—even one hour—to put your life in order but there is no assurance that you will get it.[10]

These words from Scripture and our Tradition should be sobering to us: Death is real, and our days are short. The Second Vatican Council, in its Pastoral Constitution on the Church in the Modern World (*Gaudium et Spes*), doesn't mince words on the Christian vision of death and the reality of everlasting life in Heaven:

> It is in the face of death that the riddle of human existence grows most acute. Not only is man tormented by pain and by the advancing deterioration of his body, but even more so by a dread of perpetual extinction. He rightly follows the intuition of his heart when he abhors and repudiates the utter ruin and total disappearance of his own person. He rebels against death because he bears in himself an eternal seed, which cannot be reduced to sheer matter. All the endeavors of technology, though useful in the extreme, cannot calm his anxiety; for prolongation of biological life is unable to satisfy that desire for higher life which is inescapably lodged in his breast.
>
> Although the mystery of death utterly beggars the imagination, the Church has been taught by divine revelation

---

[10] Thomas à Kempis, *The Imitation of Christ*, ed. Clare L. Fitzpatrick (New York: Catholic Book Publishing, 1985), bk. 1, chap. 23.

and firmly teaches that man has been created by God for a blissful purpose beyond the reach of earthly misery. In addition, that bodily death from which man would have been immune had he not sinned will be vanquished, according to the Christian faith, when man who was ruined by his own doing is restored to wholeness by an almighty and merciful Savior. For God has called man and still calls him so that with his entire being he might be joined to Him in an endless sharing of a divine life beyond all corruption. Christ won this victory when He rose to life, for by His death He freed man from death. Hence to every thoughtful man a solidly established faith provides the answer to his anxiety about what the future holds for him. At the same time faith gives him the power to be united in Christ with his loved ones who have already been snatched away by death; faith arouses the hope that they have found true life with God.[11]

Additionally, the American theologian Fr. John A. Hardon, S.J., provides this succinct and distinctively Catholic definition of death:

[Death is] the cessation of the bodily functions of a human being through the departure of the soul. It is part of revelation that, in the present order of divine providence, death is a punishment for sin. According to the teaching of the Church, death is a consequence of Adam's sin, as declared by St. Paul: "Sin entered the world through one man, and through sin death" (Rom. 5:12). In the case of those justified by grace, death loses its penal character and becomes a

---

[11] Second Vatican Council, Pastoral Constitution on the Church in the Modern World *Gaudium et Spes*, December 7, 1965, nos. 18, 22.

mere consequence of sin. All human beings, therefore, are
subject to death....

Death is also the end of human probation or testing of
one's loyalty to God. It ends all possibility of merit or demerit.

Properly speaking, only the body dies when separated
from its principle of life, which is the soul. However, the
Bible speaks of a second death (Rev. 20:6), referring to the
souls in hell, who are separated from their principle of supernatural life, which is God.[12]

The Reality of Death

It is important to have a healthy, realistic view of death. From a
merely temporal point of view, this includes having your life insur-
ance up to date, having your funeral arrangements in place and
expenses covered, preparing a legal will (as well as a "living will"
that reflects the Church's teachings on end-of-life issues), and so on.

But what about having a healthy view of the reality of death
from a spiritual point of view? In other words, how about the state
of your soul? Is your soul spiritually ready for its separation from
the body? For example, have you made a good, sound examina-
tion of your conscience recently? Do you do so daily? When was
the last time you went to the Sacrament of Confession? Have you
confessed any and all known mortal sins? Are you sincerely striving
to overcome any vice or habit of venial sin you may have acquired?
Do you go to Mass regularly and receive the Eucharist worthily?

We will discuss all these topics in more detail in the last chapter, but here the point is that when it comes to the reality of death,

[12] John A. Hardon, S.J., *Modern Catholic Dictionary* (Bardstown, KY:
Eternal Life Publications, 2000), pp. 146–147.

we can easily get caught up only in the temporal realities of life, which are doubtless important, and forget about the spiritual realities of life. At the end of the day, damnation due to mortal sin is more important than snagging the ideal burial plot.

To help us understand more fully the spiritual reality of death, we can do no better than to examine some of the sayings and teachings of holy men and women that have been handed down through the centuries:

> Nothing is more certain than death; nothing more uncertain than its hour.[13] (St. Anselm)

> Happy are they who, being always on their guard against death, find themselves always ready to die.[14] (St. Francis de Sales)

> Of this at least I am certain, that no one has ever died who was not destined to die at some time.[15] (St. Augustine)

> Death is no more than falling blindly into the arms of God.[16] (St. Maria Maravillas de Jesus)

> Live so as not to fear death. For those who live well in the world, death is not frightening but sweet and precious.[17] (St. Rose of Viterbo)

---

[13] St. Anselm, *Meditations* 7. Quoted in John Chapin, ed., *The Book of Catholic Quotations*, Roman Catholic Books, 1998, p. 247. *The Book of Catholic Quotations* will be hereafter abbreviated BCQ.

[14] St. Francis de Sales, *Letters to Persons in the World* 3, 4. Quoted in BCQ, p. 248.

[15] St. Augustine, *The City of God*, I, II. Qtd. in BCQ, p. 246.

[16] *EWS*, p. 91.

[17] Ibid.

THE FOUR LAST THINGS

To the good man, to die is gain.[18] (St. Ambrose)

It is His breath that is in us, and when He wants to, He will take it away.[19] (Pope St. Clement I)

Think often of death, so as to prepare for it and appraise things at their true value.[20] (Bl. Charles de Foucauld)

For a theologically sound synopsis on the subject of human death, one needs to look no further than the *Catechism of the Catholic Church*, which provides a synthesis of what Sacred Scripture, Sacred Tradition, and the Magisterium teach us on the subject. Here are some of the more pertinent passages that bring forth three important truths regarding death:

> *Death is the end of earthly life.* Our lives are measured by time, in the course of which we change, grow old and, as with all living beings on earth, death seems like the normal end of life. That aspect of death lends urgency to our lives: remembering our mortality helps us realize that we have only a limited time in which to bring our lives to fulfillment. (1007)

> *Death is a consequence of sin.* The Church's Magisterium, as authentic interpreter of the affirmations of both Scripture and Tradition, teaches that death entered the world on account of man's sins. Even though man's nature is mortal, God had destined him not to die. Death was therefore contrary to the plans of God, the Creator, and entered the world as a consequence of sin. "Bodily death, from which man would have been immune had he not sinned" is thus "the last enemy" of man to be conquered. (1008)

---

[18] St. Ambrose, *De Interpell. Job.* Quoted in BCQ, p. 246.
[19] *DQS*, p. 55.
[20] Ibid., p. 58.

Death

Death is transformed by Christ. Jesus, the Son of God, also himself suffered the death that is part of the human condition. Yet, despite his anguish as he faced death, he accepted it in an act of complete and free submission to his Father's will. The obedience of Jesus has thus transformed the curse of death into a blessing. (1009)

This is the symbolism of the three-time pouring of water at Baptism: the initiation of death in and with Christ. This may seem dark or morbid, especially at an infant Baptism, but it is actually incredibly beautiful. This death is not "death" as popularly conceived, with the Grim Reaper taking us to eternal nothingness; rather, it is the death *to ourselves* that allows us to be fully alive *in Christ*. And so, if we die in a state of Christ's sanctifying grace—that is, with no mortal sin on our soul that we have not confessed and repented for—then our physical death *literally completes* this dying with Christ begun in us at Baptism. Physical death *completes our full incorporation* into Him, in and through His redeeming act of dying for us on the Cross. What a beautiful and consoling teaching of our Catholic Faith!

Knowing this, the *Catechism* makes it even clearer to us that in death, God calls the human person to Himself. This is a truth of which St. Paul was keenly aware:

In death, God calls man to himself. Therefore, the Christian can experience desire for death like St. Paul's: "My desire is to depart and be with Christ" (Phil. 1:23). He can transform his own death into an act of obedience and love towards the Father, after the example of Christ. (1011)

The *Catechism* also quotes some of the saints who understood the truth that physical death, in a state of sanctifying grace, *completes our incorporation* into Christ. Consider especially this powerful statement from St. Ignatius of Antioch, who in his *Letter to the Romans* expressed a strong intuition of his impending martyrdom: "It is better for me to die in Christ Jesus than to reign over the ends of the earth. Him it is I seek—who died for us. Him it is I desire—who rose for us.... When I shall have arrived there, then shall I be fully a man."[21] That is, once he arrives in Heaven, he will be fully alive in accord with his human nature as he was always meant to be: living in communion with God for all eternity.

Dying Well

Holy Mother Church, the Bride of Christ, being just that—a good and holy mother—also teaches us the importance of praying for a holy and happy death:

> The Church encourages us to prepare ourselves for the hour of our death. In the ancient litany of the saints, for instance, she has us pray, "From a sudden and unforeseen death, deliver us, O Lord" (*Roman Missal*, Litany of the Saints); to ask the Mother of God to intercede for us "at the hour of our death" in the *Hail Mary*; and to entrust ourselves to St. Joseph, the Patron Saint of a Happy Death. (CCC 1014)

St. Joseph is considered the patron saint of a happy death because of an ancient tradition in the Church that holds that on his deathbed he was flanked by the Blessed Virgin Mary and Jesus Christ, his foster Son, for whom he served as guardian.[22] This is a beautiful experience that each one of us can ask for: that when we die, may it be such a holy death that we, too, will have the Blessed

---

[21] St. Ignatius of Antioch, *Ad Rom.* 6. Quoted in CCC 1010.
[22] See appendix B for a Litany of St. Joseph.

Virgin Mary standing on one side and our Lord Jesus Christ on the other.

St. Junipero Serra says, "Of all the things of life, a happy death is our principal concern. For if we attain that, it matters little if we lose all the rest. But if we do not attain that, nothing else is of any value."[23]

By a "happy" death, we simply mean the following:

1. To die in a state of sanctifying grace — that is, with no known mortal sin on our soul that has not been sacramentally forgiven
2. To receive the sacrament of the Anointing of the Sick, if our death is preceded by an illness
3. To receive Holy Viaticum — that is, one's final Holy Communion
4. To have the Prayers of Commendation for the Dying prayed over us
5. To have received the Apostolic Pardon, which also confers a Plenary Indulgence on us, provided we are open to this great grace.

But it may not be that all (or any) of these sacramental aids can be conferred upon a person at death. Sometimes death surprises us, and no provision can be made. This is all the more reason, then, to strive to live in such a way that we are "eternity minded" in our everyday lives. A simple but powerful way to go about this is to strive to live a strong sacramental life, receiving frequently and devoutly the Sacraments of Reconciliation and the Holy Eucharist. As Thomas à Kempis tells us in *The Imitation of Christ*:

If you were wise, you would so order your life as though you were to die before the day is over.

[23] DQS, p. 58.

If your conscience were clear, you would not be afraid of death. Better, to give up sin than to fear death. If you are unprepared to face death today, how will you be tomorrow? Tomorrow is uncertain and you may not be here to see it....

Gain merit for eternity now while there is time, and concern yourself only with your eternal salvation.[24]

St. Francis of Assisi reminds us that death itself is unavoidable, and that to die in a state of mortal sin is possible:

Praised are you, my Lord, for our sister bodily Death, from whom no living man can escape. Woe on those who will die in mortal sin! Blessed are they who will be found in your most holy will, for the second death will not harm them.[25]

This reminds us that just one willfully unconfessed mortal sin — that is, a sin of grave matter committed with fullness of knowledge and the deliberate consent of the will — is enough to deprive one of eternal salvation.[26] "God predestines no one to go to Hell."[27] But one *can* choose it for oneself by obstinately refusing to repent. The person, by virtue of his unrepentance, cuts himself off from eternal union with God by his own volition.

This is an ancient and eternal doctrine of our one, holy, catholic, and apostolic Faith, and is one that cannot be taken lightly.

---

[24] Thomas à Kempis, *The Imitation of Christ*, bk. 1, chap. 23.

[25] St. Francis of Assisi, *Canticle of the Creatures*. Quoted in CCC 1014.

[26] By "grave matter" is meant anything that contravenes God's moral law — the Ten Commandments — and seriously so. By "fullness of knowledge" is meant that one's intellect is indeed informed that such an action does seriously contravene God's moral law. And by "deliberate consent of the will" is meant that the person willfully does the action anyway. See CCC 1857–1859.

[27] CCC 1037. See Council of Trent, Can. 17 *On Justification*.

Death

We will discuss this in further detail in chapter 4, during our discussion on Hell, but for now it will suffice to say that while we should surely want to shun all sin in our daily lives, it is mortal sin that merits eternal punishment, while venial sin merits temporal punishment — either here on earth or in Purgatory.[28] As long as one is sincerely striving to live a good, upright, moral life according to the teachings of the Church as revealed in Sacred Scripture and Sacred Tradition, defined by the Magisterium, and upheld by the sacred Deposit of Faith, one can surely be at peace. This is precisely how a person develops a well-formed conscience.

Indeed, the Deposit of Faith itself is the "heritage of faith contained in Sacred Scripture and Tradition, handed on in the Church from the time of the Apostles, from which the Magisterium draws all that it proposes for belief as being divinely revealed" (CCC, glossary). Death, and the Church's eschatology as a whole, is part of that Deposit of Faith.

Fear of Dying—and of Living

Let's close this first chapter by considering the nature of fear of death and fear of the Lord. When St. Paul exhorts us to "work out [our] salvation with fear and trembling," he doesn't mean servile fear — the fear toward a tyrannical boss — but rather filial fear — the fear toward a tender father, the fear of not wanting to disappoint (Phil. 2:12). In another epistle St. Paul tells us:

> For you did not receive the spirit of slavery to fall back into fear, but you have received the spirit of sonship. When we cry, "Abba! Father!" it is the Spirit himself bearing witness with our spirit that we are children of God. (Rom. 8:15–16)

[28] See CCC 1861, 1863.

25

God doesn't want slaves, but sons and daughters. In regard to servile fear, St. Cyprian of Carthage says, "Fear of death is for those who aren't willing to go to Christ."[29] But in regard to filial fear, Pope St. Gregory the Great says, "If we fear death before it comes, we shall conquer it when it comes."[30]

Therefore, provided one is living in accord with God's will, there is no need to fear death. As the early Church writer Tertullian tells us, "There is nothing dreadful in that which delivers from all that is to be dreaded."[31] That said, we are never to take our own lives, as the Church teaches so clearly regarding the sins of euthanasia, suicide, doctor-assisted suicide, or so-called medical aid in dying.[32] Bodily sufferings, when united to the Cross of Jesus Christ, who suffered and died for us, are redemptive and salvific.

If we strive to live life daily with a well-formed and clear conscience, we can possess moral certitude through faith that God is pleased with us. He is the "God who can neither deceive nor be deceived," as the beautiful prayer known as the Act of Faith tells us — a prayer that we should pray every day, along with the Act of Hope and Act of Love.[33]

St. Ambrose tells us, "The word 'death' must not trouble us; the blessings that come from a safe journey should bring us joy. What is death but the burial of sin and the resurrection of goodness?"[34] What comforting words! Indeed, responding to death without servile fear can also be a wonderful witness to others as we live out our duty to evangelize — to bring people to the *Good News* of Jesus

---

[29] *DQS*, p. 55.
[30] Ibid., p. 57.
[31] Tertullian, The Testimony of the Christian Soul. Quoted in *BCQ*, p. 246.
[32] See CCC 2276–2283.
[33] See appendix A for these prayers.
[34] St. Ambrose, Treatise *On Death as a Blessing*.

Christ. St. Cyprian tells us forthrightly: "Banish the fear of death and think of the eternal life that follows it. That will show people that we really live our faith."[35]

Let us heed these optimistic calls of both St. Ambrose and St. Cyprian. These great saints of the early Church are simply echoing St. Paul when he poses this question to the church at Corinth:

"O death, where is thy victory? O death, where is thy sting?" The sting of death is sin. But thanks be to God, who gives us the victory through our Lord Jesus Christ. (1 Cor. 15:55–57)

[35] St. Cyprian, Sermon *On Man's Mortality*.

Chapter 2

Judgment

And in an instant, suddenly, you shall
be visited by the LORD of Hosts.

—Isaiah 29:5–6

I have told you before, and I repeat it: I am on the
point of appearing before God, utterly astonished
to find myself still in the world. The hour of judgment will soon sound for me; all that I have done
or permitted will be judged. Does this thought
not trouble you? I tremble, but with confidence
I throw myself upon Divine Providence.[36]

—Very Reverend Father Jean Baptiste Rauzan, founder of
the Fathers of Mercy

[36] Fr. A. De La Porte, SPM, *The Life of the Very Reverend Father Jean Baptiste Rauzan*, Branigan translation (unpublished manuscript in the private library of the Fathers of Mercy), bk. 5, p. 42.

W hen the Church lists Judgment as the second of the Four Last Things, it refers to both the Particular and General Judgments. The Particular Judgment is "the eternal retribution received by each soul at the moment of death, in accordance with that person's faith and works." (CCC, glossary). The General Judgment, on the other hand, refers to the end of time, at Christ's Second Coming, when all will be revealed and our Particular Judgment will be ratified for all to see and to understand. Just prior to this ratification, all bodies that have died will rise from the dead and reunite with their souls. This General or "Last" Judgment is

> God's triumph over the revolt of evil, after the final cosmic upheaval of this passing world. Preceded by the resurrection of the dead, it will coincide with the Second Coming of Christ in glory at the end of time, disclose good and evil, and reveal the meaning of salvation history and the providence of God by which justice has triumphed over evil. (CCC, glossary)

Numerous passages in both the Old and New Testaments confirm the reality of Judgment. St. Paul writes to the church in Corinth: "For we must all appear before the judgment seat of Christ, so that each one may receive good or evil, according to what he has done in the body" (2 Cor. 5:10). And in the Acts of the Apostles we read that "[God] commands all men everywhere to repent, because he has fixed a day on which he will judge the world in righteousness" (Acts 17:30–31). Other biblical passages regarding Judgment include the following:

> "They will see the Son of man coming on the clouds of Heaven with power and great glory. (Matt. 24:30)

> Let your loins be girded and your lamps burning, and be like men who are waiting for their master to come home from the marriage feast. (Luke 12:35–36)

> Watch therefore, for you do not know on what day your Lord is coming. (Matt. 24:42)

> A day of wrath is that day, a day of distress and anguish, a day of ruin and devastation, a day of darkness and gloom, a day of clouds and thick darkness.... For a full, yea, sudden end he will make of all the inhabitants of the earth. (Zeph. 1:15, 18)

These quotes from Sacred Scripture on the reality of Judgment and the Coming of Christ at the end of time should inspire in each of us a great sense of urgency. We do not want to die unready like Cesare Borgia, the son of Pope Alexander VI, who was killed at the siege of the Castle of Biano in 1507. His last words were simply, "I die unprepared."[37] Rather, as we said in the last chapter, we want to aspire to a holy and blessed death. As the First Letter to the Corinthians exhorts us: "Come to your right mind, and sin no more" (15:34).

---

[37] BCQ, p. 520.

Judgment

The Particular Judgment

"Truly, I say to you, today you will be with me in Paradise" (Luke 23:43).

Let us now consider the wisdom of the Church and the saints handed down to us through the ages regarding the Particular Judgment of each soul:

> Judgment cannot be pronounced on a man until he has run his course of life.[38] (St. Thomas Aquinas)

> We must busy ourselves with preparations for our departure from this world. For even if the day when the whole world ends never overtakes us, the end of each of us is right at the door.[39] (St. John Chrysostom)

> All things have an end, and two things, life and death, are side by side set before us, and each man will go *to his own place*."[40] (St. Ignatius of Antioch)

> Everyone — past, present, and future — will be judged.... Now, then, is the time for mercy, while the time to come will be the time for justice only. For that reason, the present time is ours, but the future time will be God's only."[41] (St. Thomas Aquinas)

Now, at the moment of death, we want our judgment to be one of salvation, not of reprobation. The *Catechism of the Catholic Church* begins its exploration of the statement "I believe in life everlasting" in the Nicene Creed like this: "The Christian who

---

[38] St. Thomas Aquinas, *Summa Theologica*, III, Q. 59, art. 5.
[39] DQS, p. 129.
[40] St. Ignatius of Antioch, *Letter to the Magnesians*.
[41] DQS, p. 129.

unites his own death to that of Jesus views it as a step towards Him and an entrance into everlasting life" (1020). Indeed, as we discussed in our first chapter, our physical death *completes* the dying with Christ that was initiated in Baptism. To die in Christ means to die in a state of sanctifying grace — and it means salvation.

One can enter Heaven either immediately at death, or following a period of purification of temporal punishment in Purgatory. According to this time-honored doctrine of our Catholic Faith:

> Death puts an end to human life as the time open to either accepting or rejecting the divine grace manifested in Christ (cf. 2 Tim. 1:9–10). The New Testament speaks of judgment primarily in its aspect of the final encounter with Christ in his second coming, but also repeatedly affirms that each will be rewarded immediately after death in accordance with his works and faith. The parable of the poor man Lazarus and the words of Christ on the cross to the good thief, as well as other New Testament texts speak of a final destiny of the soul — a destiny which can be different for some and for others (cf. Luke 16:22; 22:43; Matt. 16:26; 2 Cor. 5:8; Phil. 1:23; Heb. 9:27; 12:23).
>
> Each man receives his eternal retribution in his immortal soul at the very moment of his death, in a particular judgment that refers his life to Christ: either entrance into the blessedness of heaven — through a purification (cf. Council of Lyons II [1274]: DS 857–858; Council of Florence [1439]: DS 1304–1306; Council of Trent [1563]: DS 1820) or immediately (cf. Benedict XII, *Benedictus Deus* [1336]: DS 1000–1001; John XXII, *Ne super his* [1334]: DS 990) — or immediate and everlasting damnation (cf. Benedict XII, *Benedictus Deus* [1336]: DS 1002) (CCC 1021–1022, emphasis added).

In my travels doing missionary preaching, I have been amazed at how many Catholics do not realize that the Church teaches that it is very possible to go straight to Heaven when one dies. These folks believe that Purgatory is "a must," and that immediate entrance into Heaven is therefore impossible. But this is not the case, and it shows how badly we have veered away from a sound understanding of the Church's eschatology.

Purgatory is only about one thing: the need for temporal punishment for already forgiven mortal and venial sin that has not yet been *atoned for* at the time of death. But if we have *already atoned for* this temporal punishment, then there is no need to go to Purgatory.

Temporal punishment is the "purification of the unhealthy attachment to creatures, which is a consequence of sin that perdures even after death. We must be purified either during our earthly life through prayer and a conversion which comes from fervent charity, or after death in purgatory" (CCC, glossary). So, temporal punishment can be fulfilled (that is, satisfied) either on earth or in Purgatory. Eternal punishment, on the other hand, can be fulfilled only in Hell. This form of punishment is "the penalty for unrepented mortal sin, separating the sinner from communion with God for all eternity; [it is] the condemnation of the unrepentant sinner to hell" (CCC, glossary)

For my part, I don't want to go to Purgatory. Who in their right mind would want to? Yes, Purgatory is a very merciful doctrine—an opportunity God gives us to enter Heaven with a radiance deserving of His eternity. It is the "ante-chamber to Heaven"—and all souls in Purgatory will eventually receive Eternal Beatitude in Heaven, as they are assured salvation. But I still don't want to go there! We should possess the firm conviction of faith that, first, God wants us to be saved and, second, that He wants us to go to Heaven *immediately* upon death. In other words, this is God's "Plan

A" for us; "Plan B" is to enter Heaven through prior purification in Purgatory.

But if that prior purification can be satisfied here on earth, then that's where I want to fulfill it. Whether it is fixing a flat tire on a busy Interstate, enduring a serious illness, or experiencing a sudden tragedy, I pray for the heroic virtue to be able to bear steadfastly all forms of suffering, so that through this I might fulfill any and all temporal punishment while still living here on earth. Indeed, we should view all suffering and tribulation that we endure on earth as redemptive and salvific—united to the Cross of our Savior, Jesus Christ. This is what we mean when we say to "offer up" our challenges to Christ. Here are two Scriptural passages that help remind me of the importance to make frequent and firm resolutions to embrace suffering here on earth:

> Blessed is the man who endures trial, for when he has stood the test he will receive the crown of life which God has promised to those who love him. (James 1:12)

> But rejoice in so far as you share Christ's sufferings, that you may also rejoice and be glad when his glory is revealed. If you are reproached for the name of Christ, you are blessed, because the spirit of glory and of God rests upon you. (1 Pet. 4:13–14)

The Wages of Sin and the Beauty of Love

Now, why does temporal punishment remain after a person has received absolution for his or her sins? Sin, the Church teaches, has a "double consequence"—it both damages our relationship with God and creates an unhealthy attachment to the things of this world (see CCC 1472). For example, let's say I rob a bank and immediately spend all the money. The next day, however, I tell the bank owner I'm very sorry, and he immediately forgives me. His forgiveness is real and heartfelt, as is my sorrow for having robbed the bank. But the truth remains that I still need to atone for the damage done by frittering away the bank's money.

Or, what if I back into your car in a parking lot and dent your bumper? I immediately tell you I'm sorry and you forgive me, but there's still a damaged bumper that needs to be fixed and accounted for. "The forgiveness of sin and restoration of communion with God entail the remission of the eternal punishment of sin, but temporal punishment of sin remains. While patiently bearing sufferings and trials of all kinds and, when the day comes, serenely facing death, the Christian must strive to accept this temporal punishment of sin as a grace. He should strive by works of mercy and charity, as well as by prayer and various practices of penance, to put off completely the 'old man' and to put on the 'new man'" (CCC 1473; see Eph. 4:22, 24).

In addition to embracing suffering heroically and lovingly by uniting it with the Cross of Jesus Christ, we can atone for temporal punishment by faithfully carrying out devotional practices such as the three eminent good works—prayer, fasting, and almsgiving—and the fourteen works of mercy—that is, the seven Corporal Works of Mercy and the seven Spiritual Works of Mercy.[42] We should also partake frequently and fervently of the sacraments, striving to live solidly grounded in prayer. Specifically, we should

---

[42] The seven Corporal Works of Mercy are to feed the hungry; to give drink to the thirsty; to clothe the naked; to shelter the homeless; to visit the sick; to visit the imprisoned; and to bury the dead. The seven Spiritual Works of Mercy are to instruct the ignorant; to counsel the doubtful; to admonish sinners; to bear wrongs patiently; to forgive offenses willingly; to comfort the afflicted; and to pray for the living and the dead.

regularly pursue indulgences. The *Catechism* defines the concept of the indulgence, much maligned through the ages, as

> the remission before God of the temporal punishment due to sin whose guilt has already been forgiven. A properly disposed member of the Christian faithful can obtain an indulgence under prescribed conditions through the help of the Church which, as the minister of redemption, dispenses and applies with authority the treasury of the satisfactions of Christ and the saints. An indulgence is partial if it removes part of the temporal punishment due to sin, or plenary if it removes all punishment. (CCC, glossary)

In other words, Holy Mother Church, as the mystical Bride of Christ, dispenses the treasury of merits that Her Bridegroom won for us from the Cross. By analogy, think of a husband who, in his will, leaves everything to his wife, and states that she is free to dispense his wealth as she sees fit. What a gift we have in the Church!

Again, all efforts to atone for temporal punishment should proceed from prayer and "a conversion which proceeds from a fervent charity [which] can attain the complete purification of the sinner in such a way that no punishment would remain (cf. Council of Trent [1551]: DS 1712–1713; [1563]: 1820)" (CCC 1472). We cannot keep track of our sins and the temporal punishment that follows from them on a kind of cosmic scoreboard; this is what breeds servile fear in the human heart. Rather, our acceptance of suffering — that is, our penitence — must proceed from genuine love and fervent charity. St. John of the Cross, the great Carmelite mystic and reformer, writes, "At the evening of life, we shall be judged on our love."[43]

---

[43] St. John of the Cross, *Dichos* 64. Quoted in CCC 1022.

Judgment

This truth is worth calling to mind daily as we strive to be eternity-minded in our daily living. And this makes perfect sense, doesn't it? After all, if God is love, and if the human person is the only creature made in God's image and likeness, then it must be that "love is therefore the fundamental and innate vocation of every human being."[44] This is why St. Bernard of Clairvaux states:

> Love is a great thing so long as it continually returns to its fountainhead, flows back to its source, always drawing from there the water which constantly replenishes it. Of all the movements, sensations, and feelings of the soul, *love is the only one* in which the creature can respond to the Creator and make some sort of similar return however unequal though it be.[45]

This is also why St. Paul tells us: "So faith, hope, love abide, these three; but the greatest of these is love" (1 Cor. 13:13). This is because, although all three of these great theological virtues exist on earth, only love exists in Heaven. Faith and hope are not needed in Heaven because their object, God, has been attained. We behold Him for all eternity in the Beatific Vision; there's no longer any need to have faith or to hope in Him, since He's right there! But will there be love in Heaven? You bet! Love remains in Heaven precisely because it is the very core of our eternal communion with God and others.

Purification

Now let's turn to Purgatory. First of all, it's an indisputable fact that Christians from the very earliest times prayed insistently for

---

[44] St. John Paul II, Apostolic Exhortation *Familiaris Consortio*, November 22, 1981, no. 11.
[45] St. Bernard of Clairvaux, *Sermo* 83, emphasis added.

THE FOUR LAST THINGS

the dead, especially in the celebration of the Eucharist. It was a universal practice. Such prayer would be useless to those already in full communion with God (such as the martyrs in Heaven) and would also be useless to those who are condemned to Hell (those eternally separated from God). So, then, why pray for the dead? Because prayer for the dead is directed to those who are not yet fully purified at the time of their death, and only absolute purity can enter into Heaven. This is the ancient Faith of the Church.

Here's a collection of Scripture passages that refer to the process of purification we know as Purgatory:

Regarding the fact that total purification is necessary in order to enter Heaven:

Strive for peace with all men, and for the holiness without which no one will see the Lord. (Heb. 12:14)

... so that the genuineness of your faith, more precious than gold which though perishable is tested by fire, may redound to praise and glory and honor at the revelation of Jesus Christ. (1 Pet. 1:7)

Through many tribulations we must enter the kingdom of God. (Acts 14:22)

But nothing unclean shall enter [paradise]. (Rev. 21:27)

Regarding the reality of an intermediate state of purification:

Make friends quickly with your accuser, while you are going with him to court, lest your accuser hand you over to the judge, and the judge to the guard, and you be put in prison; truly, I say to you, you will never get out till you have paid the last penny. (Matt. 5:25–26)

Judgment

As you go with your accuser before the magistrate, make an effort to settle with him on the way, lest he drag you to the judge, and the judge hand you over to the officer, and the officer put you in prison. I tell you, you will never get out till you have paid the very last copper. (Luke 12:58–59)

Regarding the reality of the degrees of expiation of sins:

And that servant who knew his master's will, but did not make ready or act according to his will, shall receive a severe beating. But he who did not know, and did what deserved a beating, shall receive a light beating. (Luke 12:47–48)

Therefore I tell you, every sin and blasphemy will be forgiven men, but the blasphemy against the Spirit will not be forgiven. (Matt. 12:31)

All wrongdoing is sin, but there is sin which is not mortal." (1 John 5:17)

Regarding the fact that such purification can be aided by prayer:

And they turned to prayer, beseeching that the sin which had been committed might be wholly blotted out. And the noble Judas exhorted the people to keep themselves free from sin, for they had seen with their own eyes what had happened because of the sin of those who had fallen. He also took up a collection, man by man, to the amount of two thousand drachmas of silver, and sent it to Jerusalem to provide for a sin offering. In doing this he acted very well and honorably, taking account of the resurrection. For if he were not expecting that those who had fallen would rise again, it would have been superfluous and foolish to pray for the dead. But if he was looking to the splendid reward that is laid up for those who fall asleep in godliness, it was a holy and pious thought. Therefore he made atonement for the dead, that they might be delivered from their sin. (2 Macc. 12:42–45)

And when the days of the feast had run their course, Job would send and sanctify them, and he would rise early in the morning and offer burnt offerings according to the number of them all. (Job 1:5)

Regarding the fact that after purification one inherits Heaven for all eternity:

If any man's work is burned up, he will suffer loss, though he himself will be saved, but only as through fire. (1 Cor. 3:15)

Grounded solidly not only in Scripture, but also in Sacred Tradition, Purgatory has been discussed and reaffirmed many times throughout the Church's history. Pope St. Gregory the Great writes:

As for certain lesser faults, we must believe that, before the Final Judgment, there is a purifying fire. He who is truth says that whoever utters blasphemy against the Holy Spirit will be pardoned neither in this age nor in the age to come. From this sentence, then, we understand that certain offenses can be forgiven in this age, but certain others in the age to come.[46]

This great saint also tells us here that Purgatory will cease to exist at the time of the Second Coming of Christ. Our Lord is clear that at the time of the Final Judgment, there will be only two options to which souls are committed: The faithful sheep will be placed at his right hand, and the unfaithful goats at his left hand (see Matt.

[46] St. Gregory the Great, *Dial.* 4, 39. Quoted in CCC 1031.

25:31–33). The latter will suffer "eternal punishment" while the former will enter into "eternal life" (Matt. 25:46).

And let us not forget that the Holy Souls in Purgatory constitute one of the three states of the Church, which together make up the entire communion of the Church of Heaven and earth. The Holy Souls in Purgatory are members of the Church Suffering; those of us still living on earth are members of the Church Militant—fighting the good fight of faith, as our sacrament of Confirmation makes us "soldiers" of Christ—and those souls already in Heaven are members of the Church Triumphant. Also, let us remember that our prayer for the Holy Souls in Purgatory "is capable not only of helping them, but also of making their intercession for us effective." (CCC 958).

The General Judgment

"Christ, having been offered once to bear the sins of many, will appear a second time, not to deal with sin but to save those who are eagerly waiting for him" (Heb. 9:28).

Let us now turn to Church teaching on the General Judgment of each soul. The Church teaches that at the Second Coming of Christ, the General Judgment will ratify the Particular Judgment of every soul. Pietro Cardinal Gasparri tells us:

> Immediately after death the soul stands before the tribunal of Christ, to face the Particular Judgment.... At the Particular Judgment, the soul will be judged about every single thing—its thoughts, words, deeds, omissions, and commissions. The sentence then passed on to the soul will be ratified at the General, that is the Last, Judgment when it will be made publicly manifest.[47]

---

[47] Pietro Cardinal Gasparri, *The Catholic Catechism* (New York: P. J. Kenedy and Sons, 1932), pp. 235–236.

And St. Justin Martyr provides us with a clear teaching that there is, indeed, a General Judgment of each soul that comes at the end of time:

> The prophets have foretold two Comings of Christ: the one, which has already taken place, was that of a dishonored and suffering God-Man; the other Coming will take place, as it is predicted, when He shall gloriously come from Heaven with His angelic army, when He shall also raise to life the bodies of all the men that ever were, shall cloak the worthy with immortality, and shall relegate the wicked, subject to sensible pain for all eternity, into the eternal fire with evil demons.[48]

One passage of Scripture that conveys both the reality of the Second Coming of Christ and the hope of being saved is from the First Letter of St. Peter: "Set your hope fully upon the grace that is coming to you at the revelation of Jesus Christ" (1 Pet. 1:13). This "revelation of Jesus Christ" to which St. Peter refers is His Second Coming at the end of this age, when Jesus Christ will "reveal" Himself as the Just Judge; this event will also include the resurrection of all the dead—both the saved and the damned—whose bodies will be reunited to their souls at that time. These events will precede the General Judgment of all. According to the *Catechism*:

> The resurrection of all the dead, "of both the just and the unjust" (Acts 24:15), will precede the Last Judgment. This will be "the hour when all who are in the tombs will hear [the Son of Man's] voice and come forth, those who have done good, to the resurrection of life, and those who have

---

[48] St. Justin Martyr, *First Apology*, 52.

done evil, to the resurrection of judgment" (John 5:28–29). Then Christ will come "in his glory, and all the angels with him.... Before him will be gathered all the nations and he will separate them one from another as a shepherd separates the sheep from the goats, and he will place the sheep at his right hand, but the goats at the left.... And they will go away into eternal punishment, but the righteous into eternal life" (Matt. 25:31–32, 46). (CCC 1038)

And at this time, all will see their life, as it was lived, placed before the Just Judge:

> In the presence of Christ, who is Truth itself, the truth of each man's relationship with God will be laid bare (cf. John 12:49). The Last Judgment will reveal even to its furthest consequences the good that each person has done or failed to do during his earthly life. (CCC 1039)

And every soul "will be laid bare"—the good and the evil, the sins of commission and the sins of omission—for all to see. As we read in Hebrews, "Nothing is concealed from him; all lies bare and exposed to the eyes of him to whom we must render an account" (Heb. 4:13, NAB). This truth need not scare us if we have repented, *for that very repentance brings us the mercy of God*, and so our souls will show forth the greatness of God's work in our lives rather than the decrepitude of sin. For those who *do repent* of their past sins, the Lord God tells the prophet Zephaniah: "On that day you shall not be put to shame because of the deeds by which you have rebelled against me" (3:11).

But for those who do not repent, the exposure of their souls will lead to embarrassment, torment, and ridicule. This is why St. Augustine teaches us, quoting Scripture, "All that the wicked do is recorded and ... when 'our God comes He does not keep silence.'"[49] In other words, everyone's misdeeds will be made manifest to everyone else.

But so will our works of charity and kindness, and we will be blessed with full knowledge of the fruits of those actions. As the *Catechism* tells us: "The Last Judgment *will reveal even to its furthest consequences the good each person has done*" (1039). This truth is tied to the doctrine of merit. Merit is the "reward which God promises and gives to those who love him and by his grace perform good works. One cannot 'merit' justification or eternal life, which are the free gift of God; the source of any merit we have before God is due to the grace of Christ in us" (CCC, glossary; see also CCC 2006–2011).

Regarding *when* the General Judgment will take place, the Church teaches:

> The Last Judgment will come when Christ returns in glory. Only the Father knows the day and the hour; only He determines the moment of its coming. Then through His Son Jesus Christ He will pronounce the final word on all history. We shall know the ultimate meaning of the whole work of creation and of the entire economy of salvation and understand the marvelous ways by which His providence led everything towards its final end. The Last Judgment will reveal that God's justice triumphs over all the injustices committed by His creatures and that God's love is stronger than death (cf. Song of Sol. 8:6). (CCC 1040)

It's important to remember, too, that the doctrine of the General Judgment is really a call to conversion and reformation of life:

[49] St. Augustine, *Sermo* 18. Quoted in CCC 1039. See Ps. 50:3.

Judgment

The message of the Last Judgment is one which calls men to conversion while God is still giving them "the acceptable time,... the day of salvation" (2 Cor. 6:2). It inspires a holy fear of God and commits them to the justice of the Kingdom of God. It proclaims the "blessed hope" of the Lord's return, when he will come "to be glorified in his saints, and to be marveled at in all who have believed" (Titus 2:13; 2 Thess. 1:10). (CCC 1041)

This is the day of salvation! This is the day of the Lord! Now is the appointed time, my friends, to focus on these truths and to live them — that is, to be *eternity-minded.*

St. Augustine teaches us that "during the time which intervenes between man's death and the Final Resurrection, souls remain in places especially reserved for them, according to each as each one is deserving of the rest or tribulation for the disposition one has made of his life while living in the flesh."[50] This means Hell, Purgatory, or Heaven. Then, at the Second Coming of Christ, all souls will come forth to be reunited with their bodies for their General Judgment. Each reunited person will go to either Heaven or Hell, since Purgatory ceases to exist at the time of the Last Judgment.

Those persons still living at the time of the Second Coming of Christ will still receive their Judgment accordingly. If these people are in a state of grace but still have temporal punishment to atone for, it could be that just living on earth prior to the Second Coming would be punishment enough. After all, our Lord revealed some of the signs that would precede His Second Coming: natural disasters, famine, pestilence, wars, loss of faith, and hatred. The book of Revelation hauntingly reports:

---

[50] St. Augustine, *Enchiridion* 109. Quoted in *BCQ,* p. 246.

Then the kings of the earth and the great men and the generals and the rich and the strong, and every one, slave and free, hid in the caves and among the rocks of the mountains, calling to the mountains and rocks, "Fall on us and hide us from the face of him who is seated on the throne, and from the wrath of the Lamb; for the great day of their wrath has come, and who can stand before it?" (6:15–17)

And in his First Letter to the Thessalonians, St. Paul states, "We say to you, as if the Lord himself had said it, that we who live, who survive until his coming, will in no way have an advantage over those who have fallen asleep." (4:15, NAB)

Don't Be Caught Off Guard

Now that we've studied these revealed truths about the judgment of the human soul, we don't want to be caught off guard. This is why St. Paul writes, "The day of the Lord will come like a thief in the night.... So then let us not sleep, as others do, but let us keep awake and be sober" (1 Thess. 5:2, 6). In short, although we do not know when our Particular Judgment or General Judgment will come, we can surely work on being prepared for both.

So, how much did you think about your Particular Judgment this week? The General Judgment? What about the Second Coming of Christ? Although we don't want to have a morbid obsession with these topics, we do want to have a healthy understanding and appreciation of them. For example, I once read a meditation that suggested that it is reasonable for us to ask God for the grace to think about these topics at least as often as Jesus Christ and His Bride, the Church, think about them.

Through His Word and through the Sacred Liturgy, Jesus is frequently telling us that He is coming again. For example, we hear the message of the Second Coming of Christ multiple times throughout Holy Mass—*next time you're at Mass, take special note of the Eucharistic Prayer used by the celebrant*—and even more so if certain prayers and readings are used. Even the Gospel reading might refer to the Second Coming of Christ or the reality of Judgment. Our Lord and the Church place these doctrinal themes before us quite frequently. Let us be attentive to them.

So, if you haven't recently thought about the General Judgment—or at least your own Particular Judgment—then you are probably going to be caught off guard. If this is the case, it's not because Our Lord and His Church have not been warning you. St. Paul tells us clearly, "But you are not in darkness, brethren, for that day to surprise you like a thief. For you are all sons of light and sons of the day; we are not of the night or of darkness" (1 Thess. 5:4–5).

Apart from the Sacred Liturgy, another way to train yourself to think frequently of the reality of Judgment is to witness about it to others. Share and spread this Good News of salvation today, as *the message of salvation is indeed about today*, for no one knows the day or the hour of the Lord's Coming, and so we must always be vigilant and keep watch.

Some passages from Scripture that express this theme include these:

Now is the acceptable time; behold, now is the day of salvation. (2 Cor. 6:2)

Encourage each other while it is still today. (see Heb. 3:13)

This is the day the LORD has made; let us rejoice and be glad in it. (Ps. 118:24)

Today if you should hear his voice, harden not your hearts. (see Heb. 4:7)

THE FOUR LAST THINGS

When it comes to the message of salvation, my dear friends, it's important to embrace it in the *here and now*; this is the "sacrament of the present moment." Share this great news, and then wait, daily, in "blessed hope" for the "coming of our Savior, Jesus Christ"—words that we hear at every Mass right after we pray the Lord's Prayer.

My dear friends, one's private, Particular Judgment and one's public, General Judgment are real events. They're going to happen. It's a fact. Divine revelation makes this all too clear. So do not be caught off guard.

Be prepared and stand ready, as Sacred Scripture exhorts us: "In this is love perfected with us, that we may have confidence for the day of judgment" (1 John 4:17). The word "confidence" comes from the Latin roots *con* and *fide*, meaning "with faith." In other words, to have confidence in something is precisely to have faith in it—in this case, to have faith that God will judge us honestly and mercifully.

And let us remember that, if we live our lives in such a way that we are always ready to die and to meet our Savior, then there is no need to fear; we only have reason to love and to keep on loving both God and neighbor because real love banishes all fear, as 1 John 4:18–19 tells us: "There is no fear in love, but perfect love casts out fear. For fear has to do with punishment, and he who fears is not perfected in love. We love, because He first loved us." If we live our lives in such a way that we are always ready to die with confidence in God's love for us, then we can cast out all fear.

A simple, daily prayer that can help us foster this faith-filled sentiment is this:

> *Heavenly Father, through Your Son and in the Holy*
> *Spirit, I ask You to help me always to live and love in*

Judgment

such a way that I will always be ready to meet Jesus Christ, Your Son, when He comes at my Particular Judgment and again at the General Judgment. Amen.

With these prayerful sentiments in mind, let us now look at the great reward that awaits those who indeed remain faithful to God: Heaven, the third of the Four Last Things.

Chapter 3

Heaven

◆——————◆——————◆

What no eye has seen, nor ear heard, nor
the heart of man conceived, what God
has prepared for those who love him.

—1 Corinthians 2:9

What an honor, what happiness to depart joyfully
from this world, to go forth in glory from the anguish and pain, in one moment to close the eyes that
looked on the world of men and in the next to open
them at once to look on God and Christ! The speed
of this joyous departure! You are suddenly withdrawn
from earth to find yourself in the kingdom of heaven.

—St. Cyprian, *Treatise to Fortunatus*

eaven is our goal, plain and simple. This is the culmination of our Faith: God has created us to share eternal communion with Him. He desires our salvation. As St. Paul tells the church at Thessalonica, "God has not destined us for wrath, but to obtain salvation through our Lord Jesus Christ" (1 Thess. 5:9). And to the church at Corinth he writes: "For we know that if the earthly tent we live in is destroyed, we have a building from God, a house not made with hands, eternal in the heavens" (2 Cor. 5:1). The book of Revelation tells us, "Blessed are the dead who die in the Lord" (14:13). In other words, happy are those who die in a state of sanctifying grace and who are thus assured Heaven.

Visions of Heaven

Let us first examine some beautiful words on the absolute happiness and perfection that awaits us in Heaven. St. Paul tells the Colossians, "For in [Christ] the whole fulness of deity dwells bodily, and you have come to fulness of life in him, who is the head of all rule and authority" (2:9–10). Being in a state of sanctifying grace makes us participators in God's own divine life. St. Luke the Evangelist records Jesus saying that His Father "is not God of the dead, but of the living; for all live to him" (20:38). The psalmist writes, "How lovely is thy dwelling place, O LORD of hosts! My soul longs, yea, faints for the courts of the Lord" (Ps. 84:1–2).

THE FOUR LAST THINGS

Heaven is indeed our ultimate home, and it is there that we find our "completeness" and "utter fulfillment" as human beings made in the image and likeness of God. So, it's important that we do everything within our power now to direct ourselves to this ultimate end; indeed, our dignity as human persons demands it. As the *Catechism* tells us: "The dignity of the human person is rooted in his creation in the image and likeness of God; it is fulfilled in his vocation to divine beatitude. *It is essential to a human being freely to direct himself to this fulfillment*" (1700, emphasis added). St. Catherine of Siena had a keen awareness of these beautiful, important truths:

> What made you establish man in so great a dignity? Certainly the incalculable love by which you have looked on your creature in yourself! You are taken with love for her; for by love indeed you created her, by love you have given her a being capable of tasting your eternal Good.[51]

And so, redeemed by the one Sacrifice of Jesus Christ on the Cross, all persons are called to work toward and participate in the same Divine Beatitude or Blessed End: Heaven for all eternity. Indeed, *all persons enjoy an equal dignity precisely because all are called to the same end*. As St. Robert Bellarmine puts it:

> If you are wise, then, know that you have been created for the glory of God and your own eternal salvation. This is your goal; this is the center of your life; this is the treasure of your heart. If you reach this goal, you will find happiness. If you fail to reach it, you will find misery.[52]

---

[51] St. Catherine of Siena, Dialogue *On Divine Providence*. Quoted in CCC 356.

[52] St. Robert Bellarmine, *On the Ascent of the Mind to God*.

Heaven

Recalling the truth that the members of the Church Triumphant in Heaven indeed play an important role here on earth as members of the Communion of Saints, St. Thérèse of Lisieux tells us, "After my death I will let fall a shower of roses, good deeds. I will spend my heaven doing good upon earth. I will raise up a mighty host of little saints. My mission is to make God loved."[53] And St. Faustina Kowalska, the Divine Mercy seer, writes:

> I feel certain that my mission will not come to an end upon my death, but will begin. Oh, doubting souls, I will draw aside for you the veils of Heaven to convince you of God's goodness, so that you will no longer continue to wound with your distrust the sweetest Heart of Jesus. God is Love and Mercy.[54]

And at his trial, St. Justin Martyr was asked by the Roman prefect, Rusticus, "Do you have an idea that you will go up to heaven to receive some suitable rewards?" The soon-to-be martyr replied, "It is not an idea that I have; it is something I know well and hold to be most certain."[55] Now that's confidence — not prideful self-confidence, but confidence in the Lord Jesus Christ.

Doubt and Truth

Now, what about those individuals who doubt Heaven's existence? First of all, we surely need to pray for them. We want them not only to embrace the beautiful truth of Heaven, but one day to enter into it themselves. The book of Wisdom tells us, "But the souls of the righteous are in the hand of God, and no torment will

---

[53] *EWS*, p. 91.

[54] St. Faustina Kowalska, *Diary* 281.

[55] *Acts of the Martyrdom of St. Justin and Companions.*

ever touch them. In the eyes of the foolish they seemed to have died ... but they are at peace" (Wisd. 3:1–2, 3). Let us not be like these "foolish" ones when it comes to Heaven. St. John Eudes echoes this sentiment when he questions, "Don't you know that only the thoughtless and insane consider the faithful departed to be dead?"[56]

Still, it is important to remember that such falling away from the truth is predicted in Scripture: "Now the Spirit expressly says that in later times some will depart from the faith by giving heed to deceitful spirits and doctrines of demons, through the pretensions of liars whose consciences are seared" (1 Tim. 4:1–2). So our prayers must remain vigilant for those who, for whatever reason, do not believe in salvation and Heaven. We pray for them because we want them to become members of the Church Triumphant one day. Christian love demands nothing less, as St. Paul tells the Ephesians:

> [Let us] all attain to the unity of the faith and of the knowledge of the Son of God, to mature manhood, to the measure of the stature of the fullness of Christ; so that we may no longer be children, tossed to and fro and carried about with every wind of doctrine, by the cunning of men, by their craftiness in deceitful wiles. Rather, speaking the truth in love, we are to grow up in every way into him who is the head, into Christ. (4:13–15)

Let us turn now to the *Catechism of the Catholic Church* about the salvation of the just: "Those who die in God's grace and friendship and are perfectly purified live for ever with Christ. They are like God for ever, for they 'see him as he is,' face to face (1 John 3:2; cf. 1 Cor. 13:12; Rev. 22:4)" (1023). The section continues

---

[56] *DQS*, p. 58.

with a reading from Pope Benedict XII's 1336 encyclical *Benedictus Deus*:

> By virtue of our apostolic authority, we define the following: According to the general disposition of God, the souls of all the saints ... and other faithful who died after receiving Christ's holy Baptism (provided they were not in need of purification when they died, ... or, if they then did need or will need some purification, when they have been purified after death, ...) already before they take up their bodies again and before the general judgment—and this since the Ascension of our Lord and Savior Jesus Christ into Heaven—have been, are and will be in heaven, in the heavenly Kingdom and celestial paradise with Christ, joined to the company of the holy angels. Since the Passion and death of our Lord Jesus Christ, these souls have seen and do see the divine essence with an intuitive vision, and even face-to-face, without the mediation of any creature.

What a wonderful meditation to take before the Blessed Sacrament! My friends, don't be caught in the camp of the "foolish," or those with seared consciences. Rather, follow the truth and the Chair of St. Peter, and obtain the everlasting crown that does not wither (see 1 Cor. 9:25).

In the next section of the *Catechism*, we discover the Catholic view of heaven:

> This perfect life with the Most Holy Trinity—this communion of life and love with the Trinity, with the Virgin Mary, the angels and all the blessed—is called "heaven." Heaven is the ultimate end and fulfillment of the deepest human longings, the state of supreme, definitive happiness.

THE FOUR LAST THINGS

To live in heaven is "to be with Christ." The elect live "in Christ" (Phil. 1:23; cf. John 14:3; 1 Thess. 4:17), but they retain, or rather find, their true identity, their own name ... (cf. Rev. 2:17).

By his death and Resurrection, Jesus Christ has "opened" heaven to us. The life of the blessed consists in the full and perfect possession of the fruits of the redemption accomplished by Christ. He makes partners in his heavenly glorification those who have believed in him and remained faithful to his will. Heaven is the blessed community of all who are perfectly incorporated into Christ. (CCC 1024–1026)

Remember what we said in the first chapter, on death: for anyone who has died in a state of grace, physical death is the pathway to *full and perfect incorporation into Christ*. Heaven is the blessed community of all who are *perfectly incorporated* (from the Latin *in* and *corpus*, or "in the body") into Christ, and the last act leading to that full incorporation *is* death.

This mystery of blessed communion with God and all who are in Christ is beyond all understanding and description. Scripture speaks of it in images: life, light, peace, wedding feast, wine of the kingdom, the Father's house, the heavenly Jerusalem, paradise: "no eye has seen, nor ear heard, nor the heart of man conceived, what God has prepared for those who love him" (1 Cor. 2:9). (CCC 1027)

Summing up these wonderful teachings on Heaven, St. Thomas Aquinas writes:

The pleasant companionship of all the blessed in heaven will be a companionship replete with delight. For each one will possess all good things together with the blessed, because they will love one another as themselves, and therefore will rejoice in the happiness of others' goods as well as their own. Consequently, the joy and gladness of one will be as great as the joy of all.[57]

Finally, we are told in the *Catechism* that, "In the glory of heaven the blessed continue joyfully to fulfill God's will in relation to other men and to all creation. Already they reign with Christ; with him 'they shall reign for ever and ever' (Rev. 22:5 ; cf. Matt. 25:21, 23)" (1029). This is why St. Cyprian tells us:

> How great will your glory and happiness be, to be allowed to see God, to be honored with sharing the joy of salvation and eternal light with Christ your Lord and God, [and] to delight in the joy of immortality in the Kingdom of heaven with the righteous and God's friends.[58]

Characteristics of the Risen Body

Let us now discuss the characteristics of the risen, glorified, transfigured human body. St. Paul gives us an introduction to this doctrine when he writes to the Philippians, "But our commonwealth is in heaven, and from it we await a Savior, the Lord Jesus Christ, who will change our lowly body to be like his glorious body" (Phil. 3:20–21, emphasis added). The apostle also gives a glimpse of this doctrine when teaching the Corinthians about the resurrection of the bodies of the dead:

> So is it with the resurrection of the dead. What is sown is perishable, what is raised is imperishable. It is sown in dishonor, it is raised in glory. It is sown in weakness, it is raised

[57] *DQS*, pp. 112–113.
[58] St. Cyprian, *Ep.* 58. Quoted in CCC 1028.

in power. It is sown a physical body, it is raised a spiritual body. If there is a physical body, there is also a spiritual body.... For this perishable nature must put on the imperishable, and this mortal nature must put on immortality. (1 Cor. 15:42–44, 53)

The Church receives these teachings from divine revelation—specifically from Christ's own example given in Sacred Scripture during the forty days between His Resurrection and His Ascension, in what are referred to as His post-Resurrection appearances to His Apostles and disciples. For example, when He appeared to the Apostle Thomas, we're told that He appeared in the room despite the fact the doors were locked (see John 20:24–29). And following the episode on the road to Emmaus, we're told that Jesus vanishes from the sight of the two disciples at the breaking of the bread (see Luke 24:13–35). From these biblical accounts, Catholic tradition has discerned four qualities of the resurrected body that have been given technical names: *impassibility*, *subtility*, *agility*, and *clarity*. Our risen, glorified, transfigured bodies will experience these properties as a result of the soul's enjoying the perpetual vision of God's presence.

Before we look at each one of these, however, let us recall the Church's teaching regarding the destination of the human body after its resurrection and General Judgment. Remember that all will rise—whether saved or damned. So the bodies of the just "will be remodeled and transfigured to the pattern of the risen Christ" and the bodies of the godless "will rise again in incorruption and immortality, but they will not be transfigured."[59] This echoes St. Augustine:

[59] Ludwig Ott, *Fundamentals of Catholic Dogma*, 4th ed. (Rockford, IL: TAN Books, 1960), pp. 491–492.

And regarding what happens after death, it is no absurdity to say that death is good to the good, and evil to the evil. For the disembodied spirits of the just are at rest; but those of the wicked suffer punishment till their bodies rise again — those of the just to life everlasting, and of the others to death eternal, which is called the second death.[60]

Let us now look at each of the four properties or gifts assumed by the bodies of the just. We will make particular reference to the wonderful book *Fundamentals of Catholic Dogma* by Ludwig Ott.

Impassibility (*impassibilitas*) means that the body is incapable of suffering or dying — "that is, inaccessibility to physical evils of all kinds, such as sorrow, sickness, death."[61] The book of Revelation tells us: "He will wipe every tear from their eyes, and there shall be no more death or mourning, wailing or pain, for the old order has passed away" (Rev. 21:4; see also Rev. 7:16; Luke 20:36). "The intrinsic reason for impassibility lies in the perfect subjection of the body to the soul."[62] At the resurrection, when the soul and body reunite, the way in which one's form (the soul) will "attach" itself to one's matter (the body) will be such that immortality and impassibility will take effect.

Subtility (*subtilitas*) regards the human person's "spiritualized" nature at the resurrection of the body. Subtility is not to be "conceived as a transformation of the body into a spiritual essence or as a refinement of the matter into an ethereal body. The archetype of the spiritualized body is the risen body of Christ, which emerged from the sealed tomb and penetrated closed doors."[63] The Gospel of St. John tells us clearly that Jesus came and stood in their midst,

---

[60] St. Augustine, *The City of God* 13, 8. Quoted in BCQ, p. 247.
[61] Ott, *Fundamentals*, p. 491.
[62] Ibid., p. 491.
[63] Ibid., p. 492.

although the doors were locked (see John 20:19, 26). As such, "the intrinsic reason for the spiritualization of the body lies in the complete dominion of the body by the transfigured soul insofar as it is the essential form of the body."[64] Whereas in our earthly life the soul and the body unite in a kind of equal relationship, in the resurrection the ethereal quality of the soul will overwhelm the material quality of the body. Thus, subtility grants the resurrected body the ability, for instance, to pass through solid objects.

Agility (*agilitas*) is the "capability of the body to obey the soul with the greatest ease and speed of movement."[65] We can see this in the risen Body of Christ, who appeared and disappeared from the midst of His apostles. The Gospel of Luke, for instance, records that the Apostles "recognized him, and he vanished out of their sight" (Luke 24:31). "The intrinsic reason of agility lies in the perfect dominion over the body of the transfigured soul, to the extent that it moves the body" through space with the speed of thought.[66] Glorified bodies, then, do not experience the limits of time and space. Although they can exist within time and space, they are not bound by these concepts.

Clarity (*claritas*) means that the glorified body is "free from everything deformed and … filled with beauty and radiance."[67] Jesus himself teaches this when He states, "Then the righteous will shine like the sun in the kingdom of their Father" (Matt. 13:43). The prophet Daniel also touches on this truth: "And those who are wise shall shine like the brightness of the firmament; and those who turn many to righteousness, like the stars for ever and ever" (Dan. 12:3).

[64] Ibid.
[65] Ibid.
[66] Ibid.
[67] Ibid.

The archetype of the transfiguration is the Transfiguration of Jesus on (Mount) Tabor (Matt. 17:2), and after the Resurrection (cf. Acts 9:3). The intrinsic reason for the transfiguration lies in the overflowing of the beauty of the transfigured soul onto the body. The grade of the transfiguration of the body (cf. 1 Cor. 15:41–44) will vary according to the degree of clarity of the soul, which is in proportion to the measure of the merits.[68]

Thus, whatever imperfections or deformities the body had on earth will be taken away and will not be present in Heaven. We must note, however, that Christ's wounds *do* abide in Heaven. Rather than being removed, His wounds are glorified as an eternal sign of His triumph over sin and death in the world. His wounds, after all, were what brought the Apostle Thomas to believe in His Resurrection (see John 20:24–29).

According to St. Thomas Aquinas, our Lord kept in His glorified body the marks of His wounds for four primary reasons: (1) "as an everlasting testimony of his victory"; (2) "as a proof that he is the same Christ who suffered and was crucified"; (3) "as a constant and concrete plea on our behalf to the Eternal Father"; and (4) "as a means of upbraiding the reprobates on the last day, showing them what he did for them, thus reminding them of what they have wickedly despised and rejected."[69] It is important that we strive never to be caught in the snares of the "reprobates" who will be confronted on the last day with the wounds of Christ.

We must never lose sight of the fact that these beautiful truths of our resurrection are made possible only by and through Christ's own Resurrection. They not only come from Him and are made

---

[68] Ibid.

[69] Msgr. Paul J. Glenn, *A Tour of the Summa* (Rockford, IL: TAN Books, 1978), p. 360. See *Summa Theologica*, III, Q. 54, art. 4.

possible by Him, but He deigned to assume them Himself as a further example of His love for us and to demonstrate the eternal reward that awaits us if we cooperate with God's grace here on earth.

Let us conclude this chapter with the words of Pope St. Gregory the Great:

> So our Lord's sheep will finally reach their grazing ground where all who follow him in simplicity of heart will feed on the green pastures of eternity. These pastures are the spiritual joys of heaven. There the elect look upon the face of God with unclouded vision and feast at the banquet of life for ever more.[70]

Now that we have studied what Holy Mother Church teaches about the reality, existence, and beauty of Heaven, let us turn our attention to what She teaches about the reality, existence, and wickedness of Hell.

[70] *Homily*, 14, "On the Gospels."

Chapter 4

Hell

Then he will say to those on his left, "Depart from me, you accursed, into the eternal fire prepared for the devil and his angels."

—Matthew 25:41

The perpetual death of the damned, that is, their separation from the life of God, will go on without end and will be their common lot, regardless of what people prompted by human sentiments may conjure up about different kinds of punishment or a mitigation or interruption of their torments.

—St. Augustine, *Enchiridion* 113[71]

[71] Quoted in BCQ, p. 426

Hell is real. And it's possible for souls to go there — for all eternity. Although there have been official canonizations in the Church's history (that is, confirmations that a soul has gone to Heaven) but no official "damnations," it remains an article of our Faith that it's possible for souls to go to Hell before the Second Coming of Christ, and to remain there forever after being reunited with their bodies. As the prophet Daniel tells us: "Those who sleep in the dust of the earth shall awake, some to everlasting life, and some to shame and everlasting contempt" (Dan. 12:2).

What does Sacred Scripture tell us about Hell? Here are some biblical descriptions, from both the Old Testament and the New Testament:

† a lake of fire (Rev. 20:15)

† a place of fiery coals, burning sulfur, and scorching wind (Ps. 11:6)

† a place of devouring fire (Isa. 33:14)

† a furnace of fire (Matt. 13:42)

† a place of torment (Luke 16:23)

† a place where men will weep and gnash their teeth (Matt. 13:42)

† a place where they curse God (Rev. 16:11)

† a place where they never repent (Matt. 12:32)

† a place of filthiness (Rev. 22:11)

† a place of weeping (Matt. 8:12)

† a place of outer darkness (Matt. 8:12)

† a place where they have no rest (Rev. 14:11)

† a place where men gnaw their tongues in anguish (Rev. 16:10)

† a place of pains and sores (Rev. 16:11)

† a place of the blackest darkness (Jude 1:13)

† a place where they do not want their loved ones to go (Luke 16:28)

I remember reading the results of a Halloween news poll that had asked the respondents to list the things they were most afraid of. Answers in the top ten included snakes and spiders and dentists. But Hell was nowhere to be found. Why didn't Hell even make the list? Aren't people afraid of Hell? Do people even believe that Hell exists, and that it remains a real possibility for one to go there by one's own lack of repentance?

How interesting, though, that snakes were at the top of the list. Why? Remember the serpent in the Garden of Eden who was "most cunning of all the animals" (Genesis 3:1, NAB). Indeed, the devil is cunning. And he wants nothing more than for human persons made in the image and likeness of God to forget about the reality of Hell, thus threatening their eternal salvation. At the beginning of the nineteenth century, Fr. Jean Baptiste Rauzan, founder of the Fathers of Mercy wrote: "In our century — so proud of its insights — we see a multitude of men, born Catholic, who live without faith, without hope of future goods, without fear of eternal punishment, without God."[72]

---

[72] Fr. A. De La Porte, SPM, *The Life of the Very Reverend Father Jean Baptiste Rauzan*, Quinn translation (unpublished manuscript in the private library of the Fathers of Mercy), p. 34.

No Time Like the Present

Souls condemned to Hell by their own doing will be banished forever to that place over whose gate Dante imagined the famous warning: "Relinquish all hope, ye who enter here."[73] And St. Benedict didn't mince words, telling his fellow monks to "fear the Day of Judgment," "dread Hell," and "keep death daily before [your] eyes."[74] Indeed, a healthy spiritual life takes heed of the words of the traditional Act of Contrition: "And I detest all my sins because I dread the loss of Heaven and the pains of Hell; but most of all, because they have offended You, my God, Who are all good and deserving of all my love."

We are to work out our salvation with filial fear of the Lord through the shunning of vice and the embracing of virtue. It is both as simple and as challenging as that. The Word of God is full of reminders of the importance of avoiding Hell, and of how to do it:

> Be sober, be watchful. Your adversary the devil prowls around like a roaring lion, seeking some one to devour. Resist him, firm in your faith. (1 Pet. 5:8–9)

> Be angry but do not sin; do not let the sun go down on your anger, and give no opportunity to the devil." (Eph. 4:26–27).

> Submit yourselves therefore to God. Resist the devil and he will flee from you. Draw near to God and he will draw near to you. Cleanse your hands, you sinners, and purify your hearts, you men of double mind.... Humble yourselves before the Lord and he will exalt you. (James 4:7–8, 10)

---

[73] Dante Alighieri, *Inferno*, canto 3.
[74] *Rule of St. Benedict*, chap. 4, rules 44, 45, 47.

Do not be overcome by evil, but overcome evil with good. (Rom. 12:21)

See to it that no one makes a prey of you by philosophy and empty deceit, according to human tradition, according to the elemental spirits of the universe, and not according to Christ. (Col. 2:8)

Give ear, listen humbly, / for the LORD speaks. / Give glory to the LORD, your God, / before it grows dark; / Before your feet stumble / on darkening mountains; / Before the light you look for turns to darkness, / changes into black clouds. (Jer. 13:15–16, NAB)

Behold, now is the acceptable time; behold, now is the day of salvation. (2 Cor. 6:2)

And why is this the "acceptable time"? Why is now "the day of salvation"? Consider the haunting words of the Letter of St. James: "You have no idea what kind of life will be yours tomorrow" (4:14, NAB). This concept is not meant to be morbid or despairing, but realistic: We simply do not know when death will come, and so healthy spiritual living—living eternity-minded—keeps this reality in mind. St. Paul exhorts us to embrace this truth when he writes:

Let love be genuine; hate what is evil, hold fast to what is good; love one another with brotherly affection; outdo one another in showing honor. Never flag in zeal, be aglow with the Spirit, serve the Lord. Rejoice in your hope, be patient in tribulation, be constant in prayer. (Rom. 12:9–12)

Dignity and Duty

A truth that cannot be lost in this study of Hell is that the innate dignity of the human person lies in the fact that we are made in the image and likeness of God and are called to eternal communion with Him in Heaven.

> The dignity of man rests above all on the fact that he is called to communion with God. This invitation to converse with God is addressed to man as soon as he comes into being. For if man exists, it is because God has created him through love, and through love continues to hold him in existence. He cannot live fully according to truth unless he freely acknowledges that love and entrusts himself to his creator (Vatican Council II, GS 19 §1). (CCC 27)

So, for the human person to reject this love of God is a grave injustice not just to the Creator, but to one's own dignity. Simply put, eternal communion with God is lost if one goes to Hell. Recognizing the solemn truth that "God is love" and that "he who abides in love abides in God, and God abides in him" (1 John 4:16), we can understand and contemplate these words of Pope Benedict XVI:

> For if we ask ourselves what being damned really means, it is this: taking no pleasure in anything anymore, liking nothing and no one, and being liked by no one. Being robbed of any capacity for loving and excluded from the sphere in which loving is possible—that is absolute emptiness, in which a person exists in contradiction to his own nature, and his life is totally ruined. If, then, the essential characteristic of man is his likeness to God, his capacity for love, then humanity as a whole and each of us individually can only survive where there is love and where we are taught the way to this love.[75]

---

[75] Fr. Peter John Cameron, O.P., ed., *Benedictus—Day by Day with Pope Benedict XVI* (San Francisco: Ignatius Press, 2006), p. 330.

THE FOUR LAST THINGS

Let us now turn to the *Catechism of the Catholic Church*, specifically to those passages that concern the doctrine of Hell. Again, this doctrine has every bit to do with the subject of our love for God — or, more specifically, the lack thereof:

> We cannot be united with God unless we freely choose to love him. But we cannot love God if we sin gravely against him, against our neighbor or against ourselves: "He who does not love remains in death. Anyone who hates his brother is a murderer, and you know that no murderer has eternal life abiding in him" (1 John 3:14–15) Our Lord warns us that we shall be separated from him if we fail to meet the serious needs of the poor and the little ones who are his brethren (cf. Matt. 25:31–46). To die in mortal sin without repenting and accepting God's merciful love means remaining separated from him forever by our own free choice. This state of definitive self-exclusion from communion with God and the blessed is called "hell." (1033)

The great saints of the Church do not sugarcoat the fate of the souls in Hell. St. Thomas Aquinas, known as the Angelic Doctor, writes of the damned that they "will be as though always dying and never dead and never going to die. For this reason damnation is described as everlasting death, seeing that just as a dying man is in extreme pain, even so are they who are in hell."[76] Elsewhere, St. Thomas taught, "The regret and anguish of the damned will be useless, for it will not be on account of any hatred for evil, but on account of grief over being punished."[77] With these terrifying descriptions in mind, the *Catechism* continues:

[76] *DQS*, p. 114.
[77] Ibid.

Hell

The affirmations of Sacred Scripture and the teachings of the Church on the subject of hell are a *call to the responsibility* incumbent upon man to make use of his freedom in view of his eternal destiny. They are at the same time an urgent *call to conversion*: "Enter by the narrow gate; for the gate is wide 'and the way is easy, that leads to destruction, and those who enter by it are many. For the gate is narrow and the way is hard, that leads to life, and those who find it are few" (Matt. 7:13–14). (CCC 1036)

God *sends* no one to Hell; rather, we exclude ourselves from His presence by intentionally failing to repent of mortal sin. This is why St. Ambrose of Milan says, "The sinner is not cast out; he casts himself out."[78] Our Lord and His Bride, the Church, are always on our side, offering us assistance toward salvation—especially in the celebration of the Eucharistic Liturgy. Echoing this, the *Catechism* states: "In the Eucharistic liturgy and in the daily prayers of her faithful, the Church implores the mercy of God, who does not want 'any to perish, but all to come to repentance' (2 Pet. 3:9)" (1037).

The Wages of Mortal Sin

Note that "mortal sin" is mentioned in the *Catechism* several times in the section on Hell. This is because it is *mortal sin* that *severs* our supernatural relationship with God and therefore has the real ability to send us to Hell—and it takes only *one* unrepentant mortal sin to do so.[79]

One of the differences between mortal sin and venial sin is that mortal sin merits eternal punishment, whereas venial sin merits

[78] *DQS*, p. 212.
[79] See CCC 1033, 1035, 1037.

temporal punishment. Once mortal sin is forgiven in the sacrament of Reconciliation, it no longer merits eternal punishment—but temporal punishment for it is still required. The same goes for venial sin, which is forgiven in the worthy reception of the Eucharist but which still requires temporal atonement.

Let's turn to the *Catechism*'s definition of sin:

> Sin is an offense against reason, truth, and right conscience; it is failure in genuine love for God and neighbor caused by a perverse attachment to certain goods. It wounds the nature of man and injures human solidarity.
>
> Sin is an offense against God.... Sin sets itself against God's love for us and turns our hearts away from it. Like the first sin, it is disobedience, a revolt against God through the will to become "like gods" (Gen. 3:5), knowing and determining good and evil.... In this proud self-exaltation, sin is diametrically opposed to the obedience of Jesus, which achieves our salvation (cf. Phil. 2:6–9). (1849–1850)

Church teaching also reminds us that if it goes unchecked, sin can be contagious, addictive, and deadly. In the Letter to the Romans we read: "For the wages of sin is death, but the free gift of God is eternal life in Christ Jesus our Lord" (6:23). What's more, sin can even tend to become a whole way of life. "In these you once walked, when you lived in them. But now put them all away: anger, wrath, malice, slander, and foul talk from your mouth" (Col. 3:7–8). We could say, then, that "sin breeds sin"—it becomes a feedback loop that is increasingly difficult to stop:

> Sin creates a proclivity to sin; it engenders vice by repetition of the same acts. This results in perverse inclinations which cloud conscience and corrupt the concrete judgment of good and evil. Thus sin tends to reproduce itself and

reinforce itself, but it cannot destroy the moral sense at its root. (CCC 1865)

Make no mistake about it: Unless we repent, we can become entrenched in sin that will take over our lives, robbing us of our human freedom and dignity. Indeed, sin can even kill. According to the *Catechism*:

> Mortal sin destroys charity in the heart of man by a grave violation of God's law; it turns man away from God, who is his ultimate end and his beatitude, by preferring an inferior good to him.
>
> Venial sin allows charity to subsist, even though it offends and wounds it....
>
> Mortal sin is a radical possibility of human freedom, as is love itself. It results in the loss of charity and the privation of sanctifying grace, that is, of the state of grace. If it is not redeemed by repentance and God's forgiveness, it causes exclusion from Christ's kingdom and the eternal death of hell, for our freedom has the power to make choices forever, with no turning back. However, although we can judge that an act is in itself a grave offense, we must entrust judgment of persons to the justice and mercy of God. (CCC 1855, 1861)

About mortal sin, St. Francis of Assisi tells us:

> We should all realize that no matter where or how a man dies, if he is in the state of mortal sin and does not repent, when he could have done so and did not, the Devil tears his soul from his body with such anguish and distress that only a person who has experienced it can appreciate it.[80]

---

[80] *DQS*, p. 215.

And in a letter to her son, King St. Louis IX, Queen Blanche of France once wrote: "Rather would I see you dead at my feet than stained with a mortal sin."[81] The saintly king learned the lesson well; later in his life he wrote to his own son, "You should permit yourself to be tormented by every kind of martyrdom before you would allow yourself to commit a mortal sin."[82] In these two quotes, we see a literal and multigenerational carrying out of the Church's teaching not only about the implications of mortal sin, but about the role of parents as the primary educators of children. Whether they realized it or not, these monarchs were educating their young children, at least in part, on the doctrine of the Four Last Things. Because these parents clearly wished their children's salvation first and foremost, they stressed that separation from God, whether temporarily in this world or eternally in Hell, is the worst thing that can befall a human being—worse than any bodily suffering we can imagine. While maybe a bit graphic as only a parent can be, what refreshing honesty Queen Blanche and King Louis IX demonstrate for us, especially in a culture where moral relativism and secular humanism are the dominant ways of thinking about human existence.

Responding to God's Call

Despite the constant allure of temptation and evil in this fallen world, we must always remember the wonderful truth that God constantly calls us to Himself. We discover this truth in both the Old and New Testaments.

> For this commandment which I command you this day is not too hard for you, neither is it far off.... But the word is

[81] Ibid.
[82] Ibid.

very near you; it is in your mouth and in your heart, so that you can do it. (Deut. 30:11, 14)

And you, son of man, say to the house of Israel, Thus have you said: "Our transgressions and our sins are upon us, and we waste away because of them; how then can we live?" Say to them, As I live, says the Lord God, I have no pleasure in the death of the wicked, but that the wicked turn from his way and live; turn back, turn back from your evil ways; for why will you die, O house of Israel? (Ezek. 33:10–11)

So put away all malice and all guile and insincerity and envy and all slander. Like newborn babes, long for the pure spiritual milk, that by it you may grow up to salvation; for you have tasted the kindness of the Lord. (1 Pet. 2:1–3)

A wonderful way by which we can ensure that we are ready to respond to God's never-ending call to us is to partake regularly of the sacrament of Reconciliation. Never be afraid to make a good, holy, reverent Confession on a regular basis—at least monthly. St. Faustina Kowalska related in her diary that when our Lord spoke to her, He called the sacrament of Reconciliation the "Tribunal of Mercy."[83] Now, what's interesting about this title is that a tribunal is a court. But rather than being a court of punishment, the sacrament of Reconciliation is a court of mercy.

The concept of "tribunal" also had a particular significance in the time of Jesus. In first-century Palestine under Roman rule, one of the duties of a tribune was to defend a person charged with a crime—much like a modern-day public defender. Generally, a tribune would protect the interests of a plebeian—that is, a Roman commoner. So, who acts as your tribune in the sacrament of

[83] See *Diary* 1448.

Reconciliation? Jesus Christ does. He's your Tribune — your Defender mediating between you and the Just and Merciful Judge, His Heavenly Father. Jesus acts as the Tribune for each one of us as we present our guilty selves to His mercy.

Always remember this: Mercy is *who God is*; indeed, mercy is love's second name. God is more interested in our future than in our past — more interested in the kind of person we can become than in the kind of person we used to be. While He does indeed take our sins seriously — whether mortal or venial — God never, ever takes those sins as the last word. Why? Because He has made us in His image and likeness; He calls us constantly to Himself; and He is our God who is bigger than any sin we might ever commit. *Provided we show sincere repentance and sorrow, God is willing to forgive any sin we might commit.*

For those who might fear to place their sinful past before God, it's worth remembering this sentiment often attributed either to St. Augustine or St. Padre Pio: "My past, O Lord, to Your mercy; my present to Your love; and my future to Your divine providence." Indeed, when it comes to embracing God's mercy and love for us, this is an attitude that we all should assume. What a gift God's mercy is!

One of my favorite moments as a priest is when someone comes to Confession and tells me that it has been years or even decades since his or her last confession. Even though my heart is pained that this person has robbed himself or herself of this wonderful sacrament for so long, nothing touches me more or gives me a fuller sense of God's omnipotent mercy than to realize that this prodigal son or daughter has returned to the great Tribunal of Mercy. So never, ever listen to the master of deceit who wants to keep you away from holy Confession in order to lure your soul to an eternity in Hell. Rather, immerse yourself in the mercy of God.

Remember that each of the seven Sacraments confers sanctifying grace, which makes us actual participators in God's divine life.

Whereas grace is when God gives us what we don't deserve, mercy is when God *doesn't* give us what we *do* deserve: punishment for sin. In her famous *Dialogues*, St. Catherine of Siena records these words spoken to her by God the Father: "With eager love [my Son] submitted to a shameful death on the cross and by that death he gave you life, not merely human but divine."[84] And St. John's first letter tells us, "Whoever confesses that Jesus is the Son of God, God abides in him, and he in God" (1 John 4:15).

Understanding and appreciating the effects of sanctifying grace on the human soul can transform your life into a spiritual paradise enlivened by a deep, personal, abiding relationship with the blessed Trinity. As the early Church Father Origen describes it:

> The kingdom of God cannot exist alongside the reign of sin. Therefore, if we wish God to reign in us, in no way *should sin reign in our mortal body*; rather we should *mortify our members which are upon the earth* and bear fruit in the Spirit. There should be in us a kind of spiritual paradise where God may walk and be our sole ruler with his Christ.[85]

Now that we've ended this chapter on Hell by talking a bit about the importance of the sacrament of Reconciliation, let's look at some other ways to motivate us in our spiritual life so that we can "work out our salvation" and attain Heaven for all eternity.

[84] St. Catherine of Siena, *Dialogue* on "Divine Providence."
[85] Origen, *On Prayer* 15.

Chapter 5

The Necessity of the Spiritual Life

Therefore, brethren, be the more zealous to
confirm your call and election, for if you do
this you will never fall; so there will be richly
provided for you an entrance into the eternal
kingdom of our Lord and Savior Jesus Christ.

—2 Peter 1:10–11

If we follow Christ closely we shall be allowed, even
on this earth, to stand as it were on the threshold of
the heavenly Jerusalem, and enjoy the contemplation
of that everlasting feast, like the blessed apostles.

—St. Athanasius, *Epistle* 14 ("Easter Letter")

One of my favorite quotes from the late Mother Angelica is: "A saint is someone who loves God above all things and loves his neighbor with that same love—with a holy love, a deep love, a persevering love."[86] We are all called to become great saints—and remember that the definition of a saint is merely a soul who abides in Heaven. Given the fact that there are roughly nine thousand canonized saints, we can hope with good reason that the noncanonized saints outnumber—by a wide margin, even!—the canonized saints. Regardless of the numbers, our goal must always be to join the saints in Heaven. And as St. Athanasius tells us above, a foretaste of this is possible even now by living a life of sanctifying grace and growing in love of God and neighbor. In this chapter, then, we will discuss the necessity of the spiritual life to aid us in the task of sanctification, as well as some simple steps that will help us to "work out our salvation." As St. Peter exhorts us: "As obedient children, do not be conformed to the passions of your former ignorance, but as he who called you is holy, be holy yourselves in all your conduct; since it is written, 'You shall be holy, for I am holy'" (1 Pet. 1:14–16).

In the introduction to this book, we presented St. Augustine's statement that God created us without our cooperation, but He does not will to save us without our cooperation. Why? Because

[86] Raymond Arroyo, ed., *Mother Angelica's Little Book of Life Lessons and Everyday Spirituality* (New York: Doubleday, 2007), p. 163.

we are made with an intellect and a will—that is, with the ability to choose rationally and freely to love Him and to shun sin. As St. Basil the Great says, "Committing sin estranges us from God and puts us in league with the Devil."[87] God wants us to exercise our freedom to return to Him whenever we sin and to establish a personal relationship with Him now—so that we might someday return to Him definitively for all eternity. This is why the *Catechism* tells us:

> The affirmations of Sacred Scripture and the teachings of the Church on the subject of hell are a *call to the responsibility* incumbent upon man to make use of his freedom in view of his eternal destiny. They are at the same time an urgent *call to conversion.* (CCC 1036)

A strong spiritual life will encourage and support this responsibility, helping us to respond to the continual call to conversion.

Our Daily Bread

In the Gospel of St. Matthew, we hear Jesus say these words to those gathered for the Sermon on the Mount, to whom He just preached the Beatitudes:

> You are the light of the world. A city set on a hill cannot be hidden. Nor do men light a lamp and put it under a bushel, but on a stand, and it gives light to all in the house. Let your light so shine before men, that they may see your good works and give glory to your Father who is in heaven. (Matt. 5:14–16)

We need to remember that all of our daily activity, whether it involves prayer, work, or leisure, can be offered to God as a pleasing

---

[87] *DQS*, p. 211.

sacrifice to Him. In other words, we can be holy at home, at work, at church, at rest, at school, in a crowd, or even while alone. In my missionary preaching, I like to remind my listeners of the "theology of faithfulness to daily duty," which can act as a great motivating factor in becoming holy. St. John of God states:

> Each of us must walk along the road laid down by God. Some are called to be monks, others clerics, others hermits. Again, many are called to the married state. In whatever state of life God calls us, we can save our souls if we wish. We owe three things to God: love, service, reverence.[88]

And St. Augustine, too, hints strongly at this concept when commenting on the Scripture passage to "pray constantly" (1 Thess. 5:17):

> For the desire of your heart is itself your prayer. And if the desire is constant, so is your prayer. The Apostle Paul had a purpose in saying: *Pray without ceasing.* Are we then ceaselessly to bend our knees, to lie prostrate, or to lift up our hands? Is this what is meant in saying: *Pray without ceasing?* Even if we admit that we pray in this fashion, I do not believe that we can do so all the time.
>
> Yet there is another, interior kind of prayer without ceasing, namely, the desire of the heart. Whatever else you may be doing, if you but fix your desire on God's Sabbath rest, your prayer will be ceaseless. Therefore, if you wish to pray without ceasing, do not cease to desire.
>
> The constancy of your desire will itself be the ceaseless voice of your prayer.[89]

---

[88] Quoted in Bert Ghezzi, ed. *Voices of the Saints*, 2nd ed. (Chicago: Loyola Press, 2000), pp. 478–479.

[89] St. Augustine, Discourse on Psalm 37.

It's easy to think that we can be pleasing to God only by way of vocal prayer and meditation. While these are surely important and provide us with a strong foundation for daily spiritual life, the reality is that *everything* we do faithfully, obediently, diligently, and in accord with our vocation and state in life can be offered as a pleasing sacrifice to God.

The early-Church Father St. John Chrysostom echoes this beautifully when he says: "It is possible to offer frequent and fervent prayer even at the marketplace or strolling alone. It is possible also in your place of business, while buying or selling, or even while cooking."[90] So, our being obedient to God is part of our being faithful to our daily duty. In short, God wishes to sanctify us *where we are*, whether that is as a single person, a married person, as a widow or widower, or as a consecrated bishop, priest, deacon, or religious brother or sister. As the prophet Samuel asks, "Has the LORD as great delight in burnt offering and sacrifices, as in obeying the voice of the LORD? Behold, to obey is better than sacrifice, and to listen than the fat of rams" (1 Sam. 15:22).

So, indeed, the goal of a strong spiritual life is to be obedient daily to God—offering all of our daily activities *to* the Father, *through* the Son, and *in* the Holy Spirit. As St. Padre Pio states, "Do not undertake any course of action, not even the most lowly and insignificant, without first offering it to God."[91]

We can see this concept of the sanctifying nature of daily life and its activities throughout the teaching of the saints:

Everything that one turns in the direction of God is a prayer.[92] (St. Ignatius of Loyola)

---

[90] Quoted in *Compendium of the Catechism of the Catholic Church* 576.
[91] *EWS*, p. 17.
[92] Ibid., p. 25.

Here is a rule for everyday life: Do not do anything which you cannot offer to God.[93] (St. John Vianney)

Think well. Speak well. Do well. These three things, through the mercy of God, will make a man go to heaven.[94] (St. Camillus de Lellis)

Miss no single opportunity of making some small sacrifice, here by a smiling look, there by a kindly word; always doing the smallest things right, and doing all for love.[95] (St. Thérèse of Lisieux)

Such a practical disposition regarding faithfulness to one's particular vocation and state in life will simultaneously reinforce the "call to conversion" that our human dignity demands.

God's Open Arms

Let us pivot, however, back to the reality of sin. The truth of the matter is that we are wounded persons living in a wounded world as a result of the fall of our first parents, and so we are not always faithful and are not always obedient. But when we do fall — when we do commit sin or just get so busy with everyday life that we forget about the importance of prayer and the spiritual life — we need to get right back up. For example, St. Paul wrote to the Thessalonians that "[God has brought you back] from idols, to serve a living and true God, and to wait for his Son from heaven, whom he raised from the dead, Jesus who delivers us from the wrath to come" (1 Thess. 1:9–10). And in St. Peter's second letter we read these words:

[93] Ibid., p. 100.
[94] Ibid.
[95] Ibid., p. 47.

But according to his promise we wait for new heavens and a new earth in which righteousness dwells. Therefore, beloved, since you wait for these, be zealous to be found by him without spot or blemish, and at peace. And count the forbearance of our Lord as salvation. (3:13–15)

Let's face it: God has been patient with you and with me many, many times. This is the "forbearance"—the patience—of the Lord that St. Peter writes about here. Every time we sin and return to the beautiful Tribunal of Mercy that is the Sacrament of Reconciliation we experience that patience of the Lord. He has patience for our conversion, reconciliation, and salvation to be attained.

And so we, too, need to do our part. This is why St. Augustine says that "no one can be ready for the next life unless he trains himself for it now."[96] St. Jerome echoes this: "What saint has ever won his crown without first contending for it?"[97] All of this reminds me of something that St. Paul wrote to the Corinthians:

Do you not know that in a race all the runners compete, but only one receives the prize? So run that you may obtain it. Every athlete exercises self-control in all things. They do it to receive a perishable wreath, but we an imperishable. (1 Cor. 9:24)

Athletes deny themselves all sorts of things in order to train effectively for the purpose of winning prizes and awards that are meaningful here on earth, but have no eternal value. How much more should we Christians be willing to work and to sacrifice each day to receive the crown of eternal life? In another of his epistles St. Paul makes this analogy again:

[96] St. Augustine, Discourse on Psalm 148.
[97] St. Jerome, Collection Against Jovinianus, bk. I, letter XXII, to Eustochium, par. 39.

Train yourself in godliness; for while bodily training is of some value, godliness is of value in every way, as it holds promise for the present life and also for the life to come. The saying is sure and worthy of full acceptance. (1 Tim. 4:7–9)

Let us now look at some other beautiful scriptural selections that will help us to strengthen this resolve to live a strong spiritual life:

Therefore, my beloved, as you have always obeyed, so now, not only as in my presence but much more in my absence, work out your own salvation with fear and trembling; for God is at work in you, both to will and to work for his good pleasure. Do all things without grumbling or questioning, that you may be blameless and innocent, children of God without blemish in the midst of a crooked and perverse generation, among whom you shine as lights in the world. (Phil. 2:12–15)

Therefore, since we are surrounded by so great a cloud of witnesses, let us also lay aside every weight, and sin which clings so closely, and let us run with perseverance the race that is set before us, looking to Jesus the pioneer and perfecter of our faith, who for the joy that was set before him endured the cross, despising the shame, and is seated at the right hand of the throne of God. (Heb. 12:1–2)

Finally, brethren, we beseech and exhort you in the Lord Jesus, that as you learned from us how you ought to live and to please God, just as you are doing, you do so more and more. For you know what instructions we gave you through the Lord Jesus. For this is the will of God, your sanctification: that you abstain from immorality; that each one of you know how to control his own body in holiness and honor, not in the passion of lust like heathens who do not know God; that no man transgress, and wrong his brother in this matter, because the Lord is an avenger in all these things, as we solemnly forewarned you. For God has not called us for uncleanness, but in holiness. Therefore whoever disregards this, disregards not man but God, who gives his Holy Spirit to you. (1 Thess. 4:1–8)

These exhortations are wonderful and encouraging, but what if the "spirit of the world" tries to steer us away from this path toward God and the good? We find our answer in the wisdom of two great saints: Clare of Assisi and Padre Pio. St. Clare tells us: "Our labor here is brief, but the reward is eternal. Therefore, do not be disturbed by the clamor of the world, which passes like a shadow. Do not let the false delights of a deceptive world deceive you."[98] And St. Padre Pio exhorts us to "always be faithful to God in observing the promises you made him, and pay no attention to the mocking of the foolish. Know that the saints were always mocked by the world and the worldly, but even so they placed the world and its maxims under their feet."[99]

When I preach, I like to remind my listeners of the two-part maxim: "Christians are to be *in* the world, but not *of* the world." However, specifically for Catholic Christians I add a third element: *But we are for the world.* That is, we love the world—so much, in fact, that we want to sanctify it and make it holy. This is our Christian calling.

We can also look to the saints to help us live a strong, zealous spiritual life in the midst of the modern world. No matter our

[98] St. Clare, Letter to Ermentrude of Bruges.
[99] Quoted in Fr. Gerardo Di Flumeri, OFM Cap., ed., *Padre Pio da Pietrelcina: Letters*, 2nd edition, vol. 3 (San Giovanni Rotondo: Our Lady of Grace Capuchin Friary, 2001), p. 1093.

vocation and state in life, we need to remember this important point: The saints lived in the world, too, contending and struggling with the particular challenges and opportunities of their historical circumstances. If they can do it, so can we. Let's now turn to them for wisdom and encouragement:

> The more we try in this world to give ourselves completely to God our Lord by obeying his commands, the greater will be our happiness in the life to come, and the greater the glory that will be ours in the presence of God.[100] (St. Ambrose)

> We must remember God more often than we draw breath.[101] (St. Gregory Nazianzen)

> Thus death is acquired by sin but avoided by right living; life is lost through sin and preserved through good living. *The wages of sin is death; the gift of God is eternal life through Jesus Christ our Lord.*[102] (St. Pacian)

> Only by the power of grace can nature be liberated from its dross, restored to its purity, and made free to receive Divine Life. And this Divine Life itself is the inner driving power from which acts of love come forth. Whoever wants to preserve this life continually within herself must nourish it constantly from the source whence it flows without end—from the holy Sacraments, above all from the Sacrament of Love (the Holy Eucharist).[103] (St. Teresa Benedicta of the Cross [Edith Stein])

[100] St. Ambrose, Treatise "On the Letter to the Philippians."

[101] St. Gregory Nazianzen, Theological Oration 27. Quoted in CCC 2697.

[102] St. Pacian, Sermon on Baptism.

[103] Edith Stein, *Essays on Woman*, 2nd edition, trans. Freda Mary Oben (Washington, DC: ICS Publications, 1996), p. 56.

Try to gather together more frequently to give thanks to God and to praise him. For when you come together frequently, Satan's powers are undermined, and the destruction that he threatens is done away with in the unanimity of your faith.[104] (St. Ignatius of Antioch)

The Spirit comes to enlighten the mind first of the one who receives him, and then, through him, the minds of others as well.[105] (St. Cyril of Jerusalem)

Practical Steps to a Sanctified Life

Let us now turn to some practical aids that can encourage us to establish a strong spiritual life. This is by no means an exhaustive list; rather, it's simply a starting point for your own exploration. And realize, too, that you won't achieve these all in one week or even one month—and you're not supposed to. As St. Philip Neri says, "One should not wish to become a saint in four days but step by step."[106]

And remember this: Show me a room with seven different Christians who are committed to a strong daily spiritual life, and I'll show you seven different regimens of prayers and other devotions. Quite simply, we're all different. St. Francis de Sales tells us that our spiritual lives should "be adapted to the strength, to the occupation and to the duties of each one in particular."[107] Even so, there are some staples that everyone should acquire and practice over time.

---

[104] St. Ignatius of Antioch, *Letter to the Ephesians*.

[105] St. Cyril of Jerusalem, Catechetical instruction 16, *De Spiritu Sancto*.

[106] *EWS*, p. 97.

[107] St. Francis de Sales, *Introduction to the Devout Life*, introduction, pt. 1, chap. 3.

The Necessity of the Spiritual Life

1. *Monthly Confession:* We discussed Confession at length in the last chapter, so it will suffice to say that the beautiful Tribunal of Mercy that is this Sacrament is an irreplaceable fountain of healing grace for our souls. And let us not be afraid to call on Our Lady of Mercy to assist us in making a sound confession.[108]

2. *Weekly Eucharist:* This, of course, includes your Sunday Mass obligation—which is an obligation not because we fear God but precisely because we love Him. Try, though, to attend one or two weekday Masses if your schedule permits. After all, the Eucharist is "the source and summit of the Christian life."[109] You should also try to make a visit to the Blessed Sacrament at least once per week. Whether it is a fifteen-minute visit or a Holy Hour, time spent in our Lord's Eucharistic presence is invaluable.

3. *Morning Offering:* This is a simple practice every Christian can integrate into his or her daily life. After all, how do you know that today isn't the day you're going to die? How do you know you won't be tempted to commit mortal sin? It is traditionally said that St. Philip Neri spoke these words each morning upon rising: "O Lord, stay by your Philip today, because if You do not, Your Philip will betray You before the day is over." You might want to use St. Philip Neri's model, write your own, or use any other Morning Offering found in a good Catholic prayer book. The Morning Offering can also be a great way to renew your consecration to the Most Sacred Heart of Jesus and the Immaculate Heart of Mary.

4. *Daily Rosary:* Try to pray just five decades a day—a fifteen- to twenty-minute practice. You can even incorporate the Rosary into your daily commute or walk—be creative. In family settings you

---

[108] See the beautiful Memorare prayer in appendix A.

[109] Second Vatican Council, Dogmatic Constitution on the Church *Lumen Gentium*, November 21, 1964, no. 11.

can pray it with your spouse and children. You can give children a chance to participate by letting them take turns in announcing the mysteries of the Rosary and leading the decades of prayer.

5. *Daily Chaplet of Divine Mercy:* This simple devotion reminds us of our sinfulness, but also of the beautiful fact that God is always waiting to embrace us with open arms—provided we honestly repent. If you don't have time for the entire chaplet, just remember this simple prayer brought to us by St. Faustina that you can say throughout the day: "For the sake of His sorrowful Passion, have mercy on us and on the whole world."

6. *Fasting:* Fast according to the mind of the Church at least one day per week, preferably on Fridays. By "according to the mind of the Church" I mean simply one main meal and then two smaller meals that together do not equal the one main meal. It's really a very simple fasting rule. Fasting regularly can be a powerful tool to overcome habitual sin. As our Lord says in the Gospel, some demons can be cast out only by "prayer and fasting" (Mark 9:29).

7. *Two Daily Examinations of Conscience:* I recommend a *particular examen* and a *general examen* every day. Each of these should take only about two or three minutes and should close with an Act of Contrition (either a formal one from a favorite prayer book, or one of your own wording). The particular examen is done around midday and looks at a specific virtue that you've been trying to cultivate in your life, or at a specific vice that you've been trying to eliminate. It is as simple as asking yourself: "How have I done so far today?" Similarly, at the end of the day, just before you retire for bed, make a general examen of your entire day—that is, how you did overall that day in following God's will. Recognize certain instances during that day when you practiced virtue; and don't

hesitate to recognize certain instances when you sinned. These two daily examens help us to grow in self-knowledge by recognizing and admitting any sin we may have committed that day. If your sin is venial, your fervent Act of Contrition will wipe it away. If it is mortal, pray an Act of Contrition and get to the sacrament of Penance as soon as is reasonably possible.

8. *Aspiratory Prayers*: These are simple one-or-two-sentence prayers that can be said in a single breath — hence, "aspiratory." These are great to get into the habit of saying because they help us recognize the presence of God throughout the day. These short prayers can be based on Scripture or other devotions. For example:

> This is the day which the LORD has made, let us rejoice and be glad in it. (Ps. 118:24)

> The LORD is my Shepherd, I shall not want. (Ps. 23:1)

> Jesus, Mary, and Joseph — I love you, save souls.

> My Guardian Angel, protect me.

> O Mary, conceived without sin, pray for us who have recourse to thee.

> O Sacrament Most Holy, O Sacrament Divine, all praise and all thanksgiving be every moment Thine.

Pick out a favorite passage from Scripture and make it your own aspiratory prayer, or invoke a favorite saint throughout the day.

9. *Daily Liturgical Reading*: Have a plan to read the daily Mass readings for the day, perhaps along with a short meditation, so that even if you don't get to daily Mass you can still read the Scriptures

with the Church. There are several daily devotionals you can sub-scribe to that have the daily Mass readings in them, and the readings are also available free online.

10. *Sacramentals:* Sacramentals are "Sacred signs which bear a certain resemblance to the sacraments, and by means of which spiritual effects are signified and obtained through the prayers of the Church" (CCC, glossary). They can include blessed objects and places, such as holy water, shrines, and religious medals (for example, those of your patron saints). Sacramentals can also in-clude blessings of persons, meals, and objects—for example, the blessing of a mother before childbirth, blessings before and after meals, and having one's rosary blessed. These practices derive from the baptismal priesthood in which all the baptized share, as "every baptized person is called to be a 'blessing' and to bless (cf. Gen. 12:2; Luke 6:28; Rom. 12:14; 1 Pet. 3:9)" (CCC 1669).

And then, lastly, there are four chief texts that I'd like to rec-ommend that you become very familiar with:

1. Sacred Scripture: Try to read one chapter daily—roughly a five-minute exercise—leaving some time for meditation.
2. *Catechism of the Catholic Church:* Try to read and study three to five paragraphs each day. This is a great way to catechize yourself at your own pace and learn faithfully the teachings of Holy Mother Church.
3. Lives of the Saints: Try to read a condensed version of one saint's life per week. Good, condensed versions will not take you more than a few minutes. While we can benefit from reading the life of any saint, particular benefits flow from focusing on those saints who shared our vocation and state in life. Remember: The saints lived in the modern world of their time just as we live in the modern world of our time.

4. St. Faustina's *Diary:* I have a particular affection for this beautiful piece of spiritual writing. Try to read three to five paragraphs per week. It will help you discover even more what an immense gift and treasure the mercy of God is.

I hope that these ten spiritual exercises and the regular reading of these four staple texts will serve as a great foundation for you to begin a faithful regimen in the spiritual life. Again, this list is by no means exhaustive, nor do you need to incorporate each and every suggestion right away; it is simply a suggested plan of action meant to spur you on to a prayerful daily life. A strong spiritual life assists us all in staying in a state of sanctifying grace, which must always be our first goal.

Our Lord once told St. Faustina, "My Kingdom on earth is My life in the human soul."[110] What a wonderful truth! The soul in the state of grace is Christ's Kingdom, allowing us to participate in God's own divine life.

Living and Loving for Eternity

St. Maximilian Kolbe, the holy Franciscan martyr of Auschwitz, said, "The most resplendent manifestation of God's glory is the salvation of souls, whom Christ redeemed by shedding his blood."[111] This should remind us of the book of Isaiah, which says, "Behold, God is my salvation; I will trust, and will not be afraid; for the LORD GOD is my strength and my song, and he has become my salvation" (Isa. 12:2). And in the book of Revelation we read, "Salvation belongs to our God who sits upon the throne, and to the Lamb!" (Rev. 7:10). Indeed, these passages should give us great

[110] St. Faustina, *Diary,* 1784.
[111] *Writings of Maximilian Kolbe,* vol. 1, pt. 1.

confidence that "whoever calls on the name of the Lord shall be saved" (Acts 2:21).

Surely, friends, we are not alone. God is with us, and we have only to cooperate with His grace and mercy working in our daily lives. And then we are to spread this good news—including the good news about the Four Last Things. St. Peter reminds us that we are "God's own people," and that we are to "declare the wonderful deeds of him who called you out of darkness into his marvelous light" (1 Pet. 2:9). And God wants to give us His joy and peace, too, during this earthly journey. St. Paul wrote to the Romans, "May the God of hope fill you with all joy and peace" (Rom. 15:13).

Indeed, we are children of a loving God who is also a loving Father. We are a people of received promises, a people called to holiness, a people of a God who saves. So let us "work out our salvation" by being faithful to the task at hand, all the while letting God work in us and through us as His ever-faithful sons and daughters.

Appendices

Appendix A

Selected Daily Prayers

Act of Faith

O my God, I firmly believe that You are one God in three Divine Persons, Father, Son and Holy Spirit. And I believe that Your Divine Son, Jesus, became man and died for our sins, and that He will come again to judge the living and the dead. I believe these and all the truths that the holy Catholic Church teaches, because You have revealed them, O God, Who can neither deceive nor be deceived. Amen.

Act of Hope

O my God, relying on Your almighty power and infinite mercy and promises, I hope to obtain pardon of my sins, the help of Your grace and life everlasting, through the merits of Jesus Christ, my Lord and Redeemer. Amen.

Act of Charity

O my God, I love You above all things, with my whole heart and soul, because You are all good and deserving of all my love. I love my neighbor as myself for the love of You. I forgive all those who have injured me, and I ask pardon of all those whom I have injured. Amen.

THE FOUR LAST THINGS

Act of Contrition

O my God, I am heartily sorry for having offended You, and I detest all my sins because I dread the loss of Heaven and the pains of Hell; but most of all, because they have offended You, my God, Who are all good and deserving of all my love. I firmly resolve, with the help of Your grace, to confess my sins, to do penance, and to amend my life. Amen.

Memorare

Remember, O most gracious Virgin Mary, that never was it known that anyone who fled to your protection, implored your help, or sought your intercession was left unaided. Inspired by this confidence, I fly unto you, O Virgin of virgins, my Mother; to you do I come, before you I stand, sinful and sorrowful. O Mother of the Word Incarnate, despise not my petitions, but in your mercy, hear and answer me. Amen.

Litany of St. Joseph, Patron Saint of a Happy and Holy Death

Litany of St. Joseph

V. Lord, have mercy on us,
R. *Christ, have mercy on us.*
V. Lord, have mercy on us; Christ hear us,
R. *Christ, graciously hear us.*

God the Father of Heaven,	*Have mercy on us.*
God the Son, Redeemer of the world,	*Have mercy on us.*
God the Holy Spirit,	*Have mercy on us.*
Holy Trinity, One God,	*Have mercy on us.*

Holy Mary,	*Pray for us.*
Holy Joseph,	*Pray for us.*
Renowned offspring of David,	*Pray for us.*
Light of the Patriarchs,	*Pray for us.*
Spouse of the Mother of God,	*Pray for us.*
Chaste Guardian of the Virgin,	*Pray for us.*
Foster Father of the Son of God,	*Pray for us.*
Diligent Protector of Christ,	*Pray for us.*
Head of the Holy Family,	*Pray for us.*
Joseph most just,	*Pray for us.*
Joseph most chaste,	*Pray for us.*
Joseph most prudent,	*Pray for us.*
Joseph most strong,	*Pray for us.*

Joseph most obedient,	*Pray for us.*
Joseph most faithful,	*Pray for us.*
Mirror of patience,	*Pray for us.*
Lover of poverty,	*Pray for us.*
Model of artisans and workers,	*Pray for us.*
Glory of home life,	*Pray for us.*
Guardian of virgins,	*Pray for us.*
Pillar of families,	*Pray for us.*
Solace of the wretched,	*Pray for us.*
Hope of the sick,	*Pray for us.*
Patron of the dying,	*Pray for us.*
Terror of demons,	*Pray for us.*
Protector of Holy Church,	*Pray for us.*

Lamb of God, Who takes away the sins of the world,
    Spare us, O Lord.
Lamb of God, Who takes away the sins of the world,
    Graciously hear us, O Lord.
Lamb of God, Who takes away the sins of the world,
    Have mercy on us.

V. He made him master of His household,
R. *And ruler of all His possessions.*

Let us pray:

O God, in Your infinite wisdom and love You chose St. Joseph to be the Husband of Mary, the Mother of Your Son. May we have the help of his prayers in Heaven and enjoy his protection on earth. We ask this through Christ our Lord. Amen.

O Glorious St. Joseph, faithful follower of Jesus Christ, to you do we raise our hearts and hands to implore your powerful intercession in obtaining from the loving Heart of Jesus all the helps and graces necessary for our spiritual and temporal welfare, particularly

Litany of St. Joseph, Patron Saint of a Happy and Holy Death

the grace of a holy, happy, and provided-for death, and the special intentions that have been committed to us. O Guardian of the Word Incarnate, we feel animated with confidence that your prayers on our behalf will be graciously heard before the Throne of God. Amen.

About the Author

F r. Wade L. J. Menezes, CPM, is a member of the Fathers of Mercy, a missionary preaching religious congregation based in Auburn, Kentucky. Ordained a priest during the Great Jubilee Year 2000, he received his Bachelor of Arts Degree in Catholic Thought from the Oratory of St. Philip Neri in Toronto, Canada, and his dual Master of Arts and Master of Divinity Degrees in Theology from Holy Apostles Seminary in Cromwell, Connecticut. His secular college degrees are in journalism and communications.

Fr. Wade is currently the Assistant General of the Fathers of Mercy and has served as Director of Vocations and Director of Seminarians for the congregation. Fr. Wade has also served as the Chaplain-in-Residence at the Shrine of the Most Blessed Sacrament of Our Lady of the Angels Monastery in Hanceville, Alabama. While at the shrine, Fr. Wade was a daily Mass celebrant, homilist, and confessor; he also gave spiritual conferences on specialized points of Catholic doctrine to the many pilgrims who visited the shrine.

Fr. Wade has been a contributing writer for the *National Catholic Register*, *Our Sunday Visitor*, *Catholic Twin Circle*, *Lay Witness*, *Pastoral Life*, and *Christian Ranchman*. Several of his homiletic series have appeared in *Homiletic and Pastoral Review*, an international journal for priests. Fr. Wade has been a guest on EWTN's *Mother Angelica Live* and *Life on the Rock* programs, during which he discussed topics such as the sanctification of marriage and family life, vocations, and the Sacred Liturgy. He has also hosted several series for EWTN, including *Crux of the Matter*, *The Wonders of His Mercy*, *The Ten Commandments of Catholic Family Life*, *The Four Last Things*, *God Calls Us to Himself*, and *The Gospel of Life versus the Culture of Death*. Many of his theological presentations have been featured on EWTN Catholic Radio, Ave Maria Radio, Covenant Network, Guadalupe Radio Network, and Mater Dei Radio. He is the host of EWTN Global Catholic Radio's *Open Line Tuesday*.